Brett Beemyn
Erich Steinman
Editors

D0160904

Bisexual Men
in Culture and Society

Bisexual Men in Culture and Society has been co-published simultaneously as *Journal of Bisexuality,* Volume 2, Number 1 2002.

*Pre-publication
REVIEWS,
COMMENTARIES,
EVALUATIONS . . .*

"**B** *isexual Men in Culture and Society* illuminates shifting concepts of American masculinity. It offers valuable perspectives to anyone troubled by the inadequacies of our dualistic syhstem for slotting people into identities on the basis of their attractions."

Jan Clausen
Author of *Apples and Oranges:
My Journey Through Sexual Identity*

Bisexual Men in Culture and Society

Bisexual Men in Culture and Society has been co-published simultaneously as *Journal of Bisexuality,* Volume 2, Number 1 2002.

The *Journal of Bisexuality* Monographic "Separates"

Below is a list of "separates," which in serials librarianship means a special issue simultaneously published as a special journal issue or double-issue *and* as a "separate" hardbound monograph. (This is a format which we also call a "Docuserial.")

"Separates" are published because specialized libraries or professionals may wish to purchase a specific thematic issue by itself in a format which can be separately cataloged and shelved, as opposed to purchasing the journal on an on-going basis. Faculty members may also more easily consider a "separate" for classroom adoption.

"Separates" are carefully classified separately with the major book jobbers so that the journal tie-in can be noted on new book order slips to avoid duplicate purchasing.

You may wish to visit the Haworth's website at . . .

http://www.HaworthPress.com

. . . to search our online catalog for complete tables of contents of these separates and related publications.

You may also call 1-800-HAWORTH (outside US/Canada: 607-722-5857), or Fax 1-800-895-0582 (outside US/Canada: 607-771-0012), or e-mail at:

getinfo@haworthpressinc.com

Bisexual Men in Culture and Society, edited by Brett Beemyn, PhD, and Erich Steinman, PhD (cand.) (Vol. 2, No. 1, 2002). *Incisive examinations of the cultural meanings of bisexuality, including the overlooked bisexual themes in James Baldwin's classic novels* Another Country *and* Giovanni's Room, *the conflicts within sexual-identity politics between gay men and bisexual men, and the recurring figure of the predatory, immoral bisexual man in novels, films, and women's magazines.*

Bisexuality in the Lives of Men: Facts and Fictions, edited by Brett Beemyn, PhD, and Erich Steinman, PhD (cand.) (Vol. 1, Nos. 2/3, 2001). *"At last, a source book which explains bisexual male desires, practices, and identities in a language all of us can understand! This is informative reading for a general audience, and will be especially valuable for discussions in gender studies, sexuality studies, and men's studies courses." (William L. Leap, PhD, Professor, Department of Anthropology, American University, Washington, DC)*

Bisexual Men
in Culture and Society

Brett Beemyn
Erich Steinman
Editors

Bisexual Men in Culture and Society has been co-published simultaneously as *Journal of Bisexuality,* Volume 2, Number 1 2002.

Harrington Park Press
An Imprint of
The Haworth Press, Inc.
New York • London • Oxford

Published by

Harrington Park Press®, 10 Alice Street, Binghamton, NY 13904-1580 USA

Harrington Park Press is an imprint of The Haworth Press, Inc., 10 Alice Street, Binghamton, NY 13904-1580 USA

Bisexual Men in Culture and Society has been co-published simultaneously as *Journal of Bisexuality,* Volume 2, Number 1 2002.

© 2002 by The Haworth Press, Inc. All rights reserved. No part of this work may be reproduced or utilized in any form or by any means, electronic or mechanical, including photocopying, microfilm and recording, or by any information storage and retrieval system, without permission in writing from the publisher. Printed in the United States of America.

The development, preparation, and publication of this work has been undertaken with great care. However, the publisher, employees, editors, and agents of The Haworth Press and all imprints of The Haworth Press, Inc., including The Haworth Medical Press® and The Pharmaceutical Products Press®, are not responsible for any errors contained herein or for consequences that may ensue from use of materials or information contained in this work. Opinions expressed by the author(s) are not necessarily those of The Haworth Press, Inc.

Cover image by Gary H. Brown

Cover design by Jennifer M. Gaska

Library of Congress Cataloging-in-Publication Data

Bisexual men in culture and society / Brett Beemyn, Erich Steinman, editors
     p. cm.
     "Bisexual men in culture and society has been co-published simultaneously as Journal of bisexuality, volume 2, number 1, 2002."
     Includes bibliographical references and index.
     ISBN 1-56023-149-1 (hard)–ISBN 1-56023-250-1 (soft)
     1. Bisexual men–United States–Social conditions. 2. Bisexuality–United States. 3. Bisexuality in literature. 4. Bisexuality in motion pictures. I. Beemyn, Brett, 1966- II. Steinman, Erich W. III. Journal of bisexuality.
HQ74.2.U5 B52 2001
305.38'96'630973–dc21
                                    2001039132

Indexing, Abstracting & Website/Internet Coverage

This section provides you with a list of major indexing & abstracting services. That is to say, each service began covering this periodical during the year noted in the right column. Most Websites which are listed below have indicated that they will either post, disseminate, compile, archive, cite or alert their own Website users with research-based content from this work. (This list is as current as the copyright date of this publication.)

Abstracting, Website/Indexing Coverage ...... Year When Coverage Began

- *Abstracts in Anthropology* **2000**

- *Book Review Index* **2000**

- *CNPIEC Reference Guide: Chinese National Directory of Foreign Periodicals* **2000**

- *e-psyche, LLC <www.e-psyche.net>* **2001**

- *FINDEX <www.publist.com>* **2000**

- *Gay & Lesbian Abstracts <www.nisc.com>* **2000**

- *GenderWatch <www.slinfo.com>* **2000**

- *HOMODOK/"Relevant" Bibliographic Database, Documentation Centre for Gay & Lesbian Studies, University of Amsterdam* **2000**

- *Index to Periodical Articles Related to Law* **2000**

- *Journal of Social Work Practice "Abstracts Section" <www.carfax.co.uk/jsw-ad.htm>* **2000**

(continued)

Special Bibliographic Notes related to special journal issues
(separates) and indexing/abstracting:

- indexing/abstracting services in this list will also cover material in any "separate" that is co-published simultaneously with Haworth's special thematic journal issue or DocuSerial. Indexing/abstracting usually covers material at the article/chapter level.
- monographic co-editions are intended for either non-subscribers or libraries which intend to purchase a second copy for their circulating collections.
- monographic co-editions are reported to all jobbers/wholesalers/approval plans. The source journal is listed as the "series" to assist the prevention of duplicate purchasing in the same manner utilized for books-in-series.
- to facilitate user/access services all indexing/abstracting services are encouraged to utilize the co-indexing entry note indicated at the bottom of the first page of each article/chapter/contribution.
- this is intended to assist a library user of any reference tool (whether print, electronic, online, or CD-ROM) to locate the monographic version if the library has purchased this version but not a subscription to the source journal.
- individual articles/chapters in any Haworth publication are also available through the Haworth Document Delivery Service (HDDS).

Bisexual Men in Culture and Society

CONTENTS

∞ ALL HARRINGTON PARK PRESS BOOKS
AND JOURNALS ARE PRINTED
ON CERTIFIED ACID-FREE PAPER

ABOUT THE EDITORS

Brett Beemyn, PhD, co-edited *Queer Studies: A Lesbian, Gay, Bisexual, and Transgender Anthology* (1996) with Mickey Eliason, co-edited *Bisexuality in the Lives of Men: Facts and Fictions* (Haworth, 2000) with Erich Steinman, and edited *Creating a Place for Ourselves: Lesbian, Gay, and Bisexual Community Histories* (1997). He is currently working in higher education at the University of Rochester and writing a history of GLBT life in Washington, DC, during the twentieth century.

Erich Steinman is a PhD student in sociology at the University of Washington in Seattle. He has organized, presented at, and participated in a variety of conferences and other events for bisexuals and the bisexual community in the last 10 years. He is currently working with the Makah Nation of northwestern Washington to develop a course examining interracial conflict and Native American treaty rights. He also teaches leadership and team-building skills for "learning communities," and a class on ethics and identity that examines modern and post-modern contexts of contemporary selfhood.

About the Contributors

Brett Beemyn, PhD, co-edited *Queer Studies: A Lesbian, Gay, Bisexual, and Transgender Anthology* (1996) with Mickey Eliason, co-edited *Bisexuality in the Lives of Men: Facts and Fictions* (Haworth, 2000) with Erich Steinman, and edited *Creating a Place for Ourselves: Lesbian, Gay, and Bisexual Community Histories* (1997). He is currently working in higher education at the University of Rochester and writing a history of GLBT life in Washington, DC, during the twentieth century.

Gary H. Brown is Professor of painting and drawing in the Department of Art Studio at the University of California-Santa Barbara. During the last decade, his art work has centered on issues of life, love, and loss, and his inspiration has been Thomas Eakins, particularly Eakins's role as an American artist and teacher.

Dan Clurman, a communications consultant in the S.F. Bay Area, teaches psychology at Golden Gate University. He is the author of *Floating Upstream*, a book of poetry. His forthcoming book of cartoons, *Suppose You Went to Heaven*, will soon be published.

Jo Eadie has written widely on bisexuality in both academic and activist publications. He thinks that we all work too hard and is trying to establish an identity as a slacker academic. He is currently Lecturer in Social and Cultural Theory at Staffordshire University, where he slacks very little.

Lisa Frieden completed a dissertation in contemporary American literature at the University of California-Santa Barbara in 1996, entitled "Resisting the Apocalypse: Telling Time in American Novels About AIDS: 1982-1992." This essay is an extension of a chapter of her dissertation. She is currently residing in the San Francisco Bay Area and working in the computer industry.

Marshall Miller (www.marshallmiller.com) is a speaker, writer, and workshop presenter on sex, relationships, and gay, lesbian, bisexual, and transgender issues. He's the co-founder of the Alternatives to Marriage Project, a national organization for people who have chosen not to marry or are unable to marry, and is the coordinator of an HIV-prevention program at a community health center in Boston. Miller holds a degree in Sexuality and Society from Brown University and organized the conference for health professionals, "Playing Safe with Both Teams: Bisexuality and HIV Prevention."

Erich Steinman is a PhD student in sociology at the University of Washington in Seattle. He has organized, presented at, and participated in a variety of conferences and other events for bisexuals and the bisexual community in the last 10 years. He is currently working with the Makah Nation of northwestern Washington to develop a course examining interracial conflict and Native American treaty rights. He also teaches leadership and team-building skills for "learning communities," and a class on ethics and identity that examines modern and post-modern contexts of contemporary selfhood.

Jonathan David White's first lessons in cultural politics were learned growing up in Lynchburg, Virginia, the birthplace of the Christian New Right. He now lives in Washington, D.C., where he works in the labor movement and as a part-time professor of American Literature and writing. As a white radical and out bisexual, his activist work is primarily focused on queer liberation struggles, anti-racist/anti-sexist education, and union organizing.

Introduction

Brett Beemyn
Erich Steinman

© 2002 by The Haworth Press, Inc. All rights reserved.

[Haworth co-indexing entry note]: "Introduction." Beemyn, Brett, and Erich Steinman. Co-published simultaneously in *Journal of Bisexuality* (Harrington Park Press, an imprint of The Haworth Press, Inc.) Vol. 2, No. 1, 2002, pp. 1-7; and: *Bisexual Men in Culture and Society* (ed: Brett Beemyn and Erich Steinman) Harrington Park Press, an imprint of The Haworth Press, Inc., 2002, pp. 1-7. Single or multiple copies of this article are available for a fee from The Haworth Document Delivery Service [1-800-342-9678, 9:00 a.m. - 5:00 p.m. (EST). E-mail address: getinfo@haworthpressinc.com].

Since the late twentieth century, bisexuality has seemed to be both everywhere and nowhere in popular culture. At times during the 1990s, bisexuals were hard to overlook, with prominent stories in *Time, Newsweek,* the *New York Times, Essence,* and other national media;[1] TV tabloid talk shows regularly spotlighting bisexual guests; films like *Chasing Amy, Go Fish,* and the infamous *Basic Instinct*; and a growing number of self-identified bisexual musicians and actresses/ actors, including Ani Difranco, Me'shell Ndegéocello, Jill Sobule, Sandra Bernhard, Courtney Love, Angelina Jolie, Michael Stipe, and Andy Dick. But as demonstrated by these films featuring bisexual female characters and this list of mostly female celebrities, the visibility of bisexuals in contemporary U.S. society is largely limited to bisexual women.

Not only are there relatively few cultural images of men who are attracted to more than one gender, but the representations that do exist often focus on how behaviorally bisexual men supposedly pose a hidden HIV threat to heterosexual women. Stories in *Redbook, Cosmopolitan,* and *Mademoiselle,* for example, in the late 1980s and early 1990s warned their largely female readership of what one article characterized as "The Secret Life of Bisexual Husbands."[2] Films of the time, such as *American Commandos, Together Alone,* and *Blue Velvet,* and the widely popular fiction of E. Lynn Harris have also reinforced the stereotype of the dangerous, predatory bisexual man. While the association of male bisexuality with AIDS may be less prevalent in the mainstream media today, as AIDS coverage itself has diminished, hostility toward bisexual men remains. A study by Mickey Eliason included in our previous volume, *Bisexuality in the Lives of Men: Facts and Fictions,* found that heterosexual college students rate bisexual men as more unacceptable than lesbians, gay men, and bisexual women.[3]

Undoubtedly, the lack of critiques of how bisexuality is depicted in literature, film, and other aspects of popular culture contributes to this stigmatization. *Bisexual Men in Culture and Society* helps rectify the absence of such analyses by examining literary, cultural, and theoretical representations of male bisexuality. Along with *Bisexuality in the Lives of Men: Facts and Fictions,* it is the first scholarly work to focus specifically on bisexual men.

Challenging stereotypes about bisexual men is a concern shared by the contributors to *Bisexual Men in Culture and Society.* Marshall Miller analyzes how news coverage in the mainstream media from the mid-1980s to the mid-1990s characterized bisexual men as a dangerous HIV risk to their female partners by focusing on isolated cases in which a white heterosexual woman became infected by a man who secretly had sexual relationships with other men. In these stories, women are "innocent" victims of "irresponsible, deceitful bisexual men who had too much sex with too many people." Miller argues that such coverage not only demonized self-identified bisexual men, but also led to a focus on sexual orientation, rather than sexual behavior, in HIV-prevention strategies. By critically examining media messages, he demonstrates the importance of a saying that has become popular among bisexual HIV-prevention educators: "Sexual orientation doesn't spread HIV, unsafe sex does."

A link between AIDS and bisexuality is also made in E. Lynn Harris's fiction, which is analyzed here by Lisa Frieden. Focusing on his first novel, *Invisible Life*, Frieden charts the sexual development of its bisexual main character, Raymond. Frieden shows how Harris ultimately links Raymond's fluid sexual desire to notions of insecurity, danger, and duplicity–symbolized by the AIDS-related death of the wife of his bisexual friend and lover–rather than recognizing the ways in which rigid social standards constrain and prevent the disclosure of sexual complexity. In *Invisible Life*, bisexuality becomes a dubious ethical choice, whereas heterosexuality demonstrates an acceptance of moral responsibility to individual sexual partners and a concern for the well-being of African American communities. His subsequent novels continue to portray both heterosexual and gay characters as comfortable with their sexual identities and to limit bisexuals to an "invisible life."

In Harris's fiction, bisexual men frequently function as the unstable, immoral, and dangerous contrast to the more reliable, principled, and non-threatening gay or heterosexual characters. Jonathan David White analyzes a related theme: a conspicuous pattern of bisexual male killers in recent Hollywood films, and its relationship to both the previous portrayal of gay men as sexual predators and the subsequent cinematic appearance of bisexual women murderers. White sees such representations as evidence of the anxieties and fantasies that currently circulate around bisexual men and women. These images, much like the heated "bi debates" in the lesbian and gay press regarding the status and meaning of bisexuality, are an expression of the tensions present in sexual identity politics. White's analysis underscores the way that multiple meanings of bisexuality–from images of the "subversive queer" who challenges compulsory heterosexuality to the "double agent" who is complicit in its dominance–are offered and contested in contemporary film.

The conflicts within sexual identity politics are also addressed by Jo Eadie in his examination of the portrayal of bisexual-gay relations in the 1990 film *Together Alone*. Through discussing the tensions that develop between its male protagonists, he considers how bisexual and gay men can have conflicting perspectives and motivations, how each can hold misguided assumptions about the other, and why the two groups must find ways to communicate despite such distinctions and disagreements. What Eadie sees as hopeful about the film is not its solution of differences or its assertion of similarities, but its affirmation of the necessity to continue to have a dialogue about these antagonisms, disputes, and failures to reach agreement. "Bisexual possibilities," he argues, "are kept in lively motion even through those cultural clashes that most enrage us."

Brett Beemyn explores one such "bisexual possibility" through a reading of James Baldwin's *Giovanni's Room* and *Another Country* that considers "bisexual behavior" not just as sexual expression, but also as the ability to make connections with both women and men, including the female and male within ourselves. Seen from this perspective, individuals may or may not be born "bisexual," but they have to become "bisexual" if they are to break down the rigid identity categories that can stand in the way of close "intragender" and "intergender" relationships. At the same time, simply being sexually involved with both women and men does not mean that individuals can step outside themselves and risk loving others, for, as Beemyn demonstrates, two of the seemingly bisexual characters fail tragically in their attempts to relate to anyone else, resulting in the literal death of one and the spiritual death of the other.

Many people have contributed to *Bisexual Men in Culture and Society*, often from afar and sometimes without their knowledge. Foremost, we thank Fritz Klein and The Haworth Press for believing in the project and giving us the opportunity to publish this work when other presses felt that a book about male bisexuality was unmarketable, if not unworthy. All of the authors have written groundbreaking essays, and we thank them for supporting us even when it seemed that the anthology would never be completed. We also greatly appreciate the sustenance, inspiration, and support provided by long-time bisexual activists, including Stephanie Berger, Wayne Bryant, Elias Farajajé-Jones, Alexei Guren, Loraine Hutchins, Lani Ka'ahumanu, and Naomi Tucker. To them and to the many other individuals we have failed to name here, we are greatly indebted, and hope that this volume constitutes partial repayment for their assistance.

This collection began as Brett's vision, and initially it was his solo project. Erich would like to thank Brett for his invitation to join him in editing the volume. He would also like to recognize the support of faculty and colleagues at the University of Washington, especially Judy Howard, Julie Brines, Stephanie Burkhalter, and Davis Patterson. Brett would like to acknowledge Erich's willingness to come onboard partway into the process to make this collection a reality, and the important social scientific perspective he has brought to the project. He would also like to thank Michele Spring-Moore for her editing advice and for bringing greater personal meaning to this volume and his life.

In closing, we hope that these essays not only add to current research and our collective knowledge, but also serve as a resource to help men of all sexual behaviors and identities, but especially bisexual men, experience more affirmation and understanding, and individually and collectively build more satisfying lives. It will require substantial changes in both individual attitudes and the society at large for the day to come when, as a matter of course, people will embrace rather than stigmatize such desires and sensibilities in themselves and others. Bisexual men can move us closer to that day by supporting and celebrating each other's bodies, desires, and relationships and by developing a positive sense of themselves as bisexuals.

NOTES

1. "Bisexuality: What Is It?", *Time,* August 17, 1992: 49-51; "Not Gay, Not Straight: A New Sexuality Emerges," *Newsweek,* July 17, 1995: 44-50; "A New Generation Seems Ready to Give Bisexuality a Place in the Spectrum," *New York Times,* June 2, 1995: C10; "Bisexuality: Out of the Closet," *Essence,* October 1992: 61-62, 130-32.

2. "The Secret Life of Bisexual Husbands," *Redbook,* September 1993: 114-17, 135; "The Risky Business of Bisexual Love," *Cosmopolitan,* October 1989: 202-05; "Is There a Man in Your Man's Life? What Every Girl Should Know About the Bisexual Guy," *Mademoiselle,* July 1987: 134-35, 153-54.

3. Mickey Eliason, "Bi-Negativity: The Stigma Facing Bisexual Men," *Bisexuality in the Lives of Men: Facts and Fictions* (Binghamton, NY: Harrington Park Press, 2001).

In Dialogue

Problems and Opportunities in Together Alone's Visions of Queer Masculinities

Jo Eadie

© 2002 by The Haworth Press, Inc. All rights reserved.

[Haworth co-indexing entry note]: "In Dialogue: Problems and Opportunities in *Together Alone*'s Visions of Queer Masculinities." Eadie, Jo. Co-published simultaneously in *Journal of Bisexuality* (Harrington Park Press, an imprint of The Haworth Press, Inc.) Vol. 2, No. 1, 2002, pp. 9-35; and: *Bisexual Men in Culture and Society* (ed: Brett Beemyn and Erich Steinman) Harrington Park Press, an imprint of The Haworth Press, Inc., 2002, pp. 9-35. Single or multiple copies of this article are available for a fee from The Haworth Document Delivery Service [1-800-342-9678, 9:00 a.m. - 5:00 p.m. (EST). E-mail address: getinfo@haworthpressinc.com].

SUMMARY. This article considers the tensions and solidarities between gay and bisexual men by looking at the representation of a dialogue between two men in the film *Together Alone*. By exploring these identities, the film suggests ways in which gay and bisexual men can enter into discussion about their connections and divergences. It recognizes the differences between the two sexual communities, but also risks exaggerating those differences in the process. At the same time, it offers an image of unity that is equally problematic, because it relies on undefined liberal notions of "common humanity," which fail to consider the subcultural specificities of the groups of men involved. More usefully than either of these, it offers an important model of dialogue which accepts disagreement and hostility as one mechanism by which communities are in fact sustained. *[Article copies available for a fee from The Haworth Document Delivery Service: 1-800-342-9678. E-mail address: <getinfo@haworthpressinc.com> Website: <http://www.HaworthPress.com> © 2002 by The Haworth Press, Inc. All rights reserved.]*

KEYWORDS. AIDS, bisexual men, bisexuality, community, dialogue, difference, gay men, identity, masculinity, solidarity, *Together Alone*

In 1997, the British lifestyle magazine *Attitude* ran an article titled "No Good Bi's."[1] Its gay male writer, Mark White, purported to recount his brief and unhappy relationship with a bisexual man. The article passes through a series of unsupported generalizations ("If there are some honest bisexuals out there, then this must seem like a bit of an unfair rant, but most of the ones I've met have had the kind of emotional problems that would leave a therapist hurling themselves through the nearest window"), by way of various caustic witticisms ("our New Home Secretary Jack Straw has promised to introduce a Bill banning bisexuality on the grounds of extreme cruelty and savage contradiction"), and ends with a muddled series of claims, including that if you want sex with both men and women, "you're not bisexual, just horny." The article even goes as far as to urge its readers to have no business with bisexuals, since "there comes a time when you've got to take a stand for what's right and decent."

While White's piece is manifestly tongue-in-cheek in a number of ways, it is also illogical, careless, and uninformed–characteristic of the journalistic penchant for copy that reads well when read quickly. But it, nevertheless, serves to recirculate a series of prejudices that remain symptomatic of a long-standing tension between some portions of the gay male community and some of us who are, in terms of either behavior or identity, bisexual.

I want to use the term "some" advisedly here, since it is also the case that many gay and bisexual men sustain sexual, political, affectional, brotherly, or professional relationships with each other without any such animosity or mistrust. Furthermore, we should remember that while it is possible to marshal evidence that such divisions have existed for some time (for instance, Chris Cagle [1996: 53] found articles dating from 1953 making similar points regarding bisexuality), it is also a fact that they have been actively contested by many prominent groups within the recent history of gay activism (Cagle, 1996; Donaldson, 1995; Power, 1996; Udis-Kessler, 1995). Indeed, it may be the case that it is only at those points where identity politics has sharpened the apparent necessity for marking such differences-distinctions rarely sought by, for instance, men meeting for anonymous sex-that an apparent gulf has opened between us. Yet, given those provisos, these conflicts do exist. Some-or many-gay men do seem to consider most-or all-bisexual men to be incapable of sustained same-sex relationships, unwilling to engage politically with homophobia, benefiting socially from institutionalized heterosexism, sexually unfaithful, and emotionally unstable.

As a way of thinking about such hostility, I want to consider the independent black and white film *Together Alone* (P. J. Castellanata, U.S., 1990). It offers a broadly optimistic vision of the possibility of finding ways of negotiating the differences between gay and bisexual men, addressing such conflicts as: heterosexual versus homosexual desire; the conceptualization of desire in terms of political community versus personal sexual satisfaction; the difficulties of communicating with someone who does not share your location within a specific sexual culture; and the hope of reconciliation amongst different peoples in the name of a shared dialogue about the shape of the future.

These are all questions that have been central to recent sexual politics-indeed, to identity politics in general-and I take the film to be an honorable attempt to address them. However, the solutions that it offers seem to be both limited and, more problematically, conceived of in ways that replicate the wider discursive structures entailed in thinking of sexuality in terms of limitations of identity and difference, even as it seeks to rework them in some productive new direction. This is not to write off the cultural work that the film undertakes as redundant or irredeemably compromised. Rather, it is to attempt a critical appraisal of the strengths and weaknesses of its project and to outline what we can learn from both.

DIALOGUES, DISCLOSURES, DECISIONS, AND DISPUTES

Shown in the U.K. as part of the 1990 Lesbian and Gay Film Festival, *Together Alone* is a dramatic dialogue between two men, one gay and one bisexual, who have just met for the first time at a bar and have had sex. Set in the apartment of the gay man, the film's ninety minutes of "action" consist solely of a lengthy conversation which moves through a series of disagreements between the two as they examine the motives for various key actions in their lives and disclose aspects of themselves which the other had misrecognized or overlooked.

This static structure earned it some hostility: "a politically correct polemic rather than a movie," ran a review in *Gay Times* (August 1995), which concluded, "worthy–but totally boring." Its status as "worthy," as "polemic," and as "politically correct" reflects its core intention: to explore the ethics of a number of difficult decisions made by the two men–all with substantial resonances for bisexual and gay men more generally–and to offer a liberal affirmation of their respective right to make such decisions in their own way. It thus seeks both to affirm their differences and to show that these men are able to find ways of understanding their situations as similar or related.

Emblematic of this task, the film begins with the discovery that the two men have the same name, although each spells it slightly differently: Brian and Bryan. This stands as the defining instance of the principle of "same yet different" which governs the film–its belief that small differences can be resolved through recognizing the fact that all decisions are the same for everybody: hard, anxious, and carrying responsibilities. And in turn the i/y difference reflects the different sexualities of the two men: the y in Bryan marks him as gay; the i in Brian marks him as bi. The gay/bi difference is thus itself mapped onto the i/y difference: small but significant, written differently but pronounced in the same way. And it is this question of how to negotiate between differences that is central to the film–a question of no small interest to gay and bisexual men in the film's audience, and, indeed, to anyone concerned with the possibilities of living in a world which we increasingly view in terms of our differences and incompatibilities.

The film's predominant dramatic form involves exchanges in which each man asserts his view of the events that take place between them, or in his own life, and the other then challenges that interpretation with one of his own. Such a format enables *Together Alone* to emphasize its governing principles: that each man has his own radically different motives and interpretations; that each makes unwarranted judgments and assumptions about the other; and that it is important to find a way of meeting and communicating in the face of difference or disagreement.

The film's dialogue is thus peppered with attempts by one man to claim the accuracy of his interpretation–"but don't you see," "let's face it"–and with attempts by the other to refuse to accept the interpretations given: "I'm not like you," "Who the hell are you trying to kid?," "Here I am thinking I'm being totally clear and you're not understanding any of it." The conflicts between them are a power struggle over who will set the meanings of their own actions and legitimate their appropriateness and intelligibility. "What I'm saying is . . ." begins Brian, setting the terms of his interpretation of the encounter–that the pleasures of sex should be measured against a choice about real, but limited, amounts of risk; "I think I know what you're saying: you're saying you don't give a flying fuck whether or not you gave me AIDS," interrupts Bryan to dispute those terms and supply his perspective instead.

Differences around AIDS are at the center of one of their major disputes: Brian has fucked Bryan, and they disagree about who should assume responsibility for it. Brian argues that he is confident about his HIV-negative status and that he took Bryan's willingness to comply with unprotected fucking as an indication of similar confidence; Bryan argues that he gave control over to Brian, who should have accepted the responsibility for protection which that presumably entailed. Disputing who decided to have unsafe sex, each attempts to affirm his own understanding of the situation and to ridicule or undermine the position of the other (Brian: "Don't try to shirk your responsibilities onto me buddy. I would have worn a rubber if you asked. You didn't ask"; Bryan: "So it's your own fault if you get AIDS?"). Their conversation is structured by challenges and counter-challenges, producing exchanges like the following over how each should address the possibility of being HIV positive:

> Bryan: If the mechanic of an airplane knows something is wrong, or even thinks something might be wrong with an airplane, don't you think that he or she owes it to the passengers to speak up?

> Brian: Sure he does, but that doesn't mean he will. All I'm saying is you've got to look out for yourself. You can't go around trusting everyone–being innocent and naive. Trust is something people have got to earn.

> Bryan: So, OK–if that plane crashes, you think the mechanic can say, "Oh well, they took a chance when they got on?"

> Brian: He can say whatever he wants, if you're dead, what difference does it make? Even if he says "I'm sorry," you're still dead. All I'm saying is, you've got to be careful.

> Bryan: Spending the night with a total stranger isn't exactly my idea of careful. Diseases aside Brian, for all you know I could be some sort of lunatic serial killer.

> Brian: And for that matter, so could I.

Here, each asserts the logic of his own position over that of the other ("don't you think . . ."), attempting to construct his own perspective as a form of absolute truth ("trust is something you've got to earn"). Underneath that structure, I suggest, lies the tension between gay and bisexual men–the sense that each possesses his own self-contained and separate set of values, which the other experiences as illogical or incoherent. And it is this construction of the experience of these two sexual identities which makes the film a fascinating object to study from a bisexual perspective.

Besides defining their respective personalities–Brian, carefree, self-willed, pragmatic; Bryan, cautious, concerned, idealistic–the exchange raises two crucial issues. First, it stresses the ways in which knowledge and ignorance are related to issues of risk and safety: it focuses on how the degree to which other people share their knowledge determines the extent to which one can make informed decisions. Second, it connects the risks of ignorance directly to the fact that neither knows enough about the other to be certain that they are not taking any one of a number of possible risks. Either man could be the mechanic who fails to share his knowledge of danger.

This focus on trust and knowledge drives the film, which takes up these themes with regard to several facets of the two characters' lives, notably Brian's bisexuality. Initially raising it as a theoretical perspective ("you have to allow for shades of gray . . . not every man who has sex with another man is necessarily gay"), it then becomes an identity which he claims ("I'd say I was a three or a four on the [Kinsey] scale"), and finally a concrete way of life ("I'm married with a kid").

For Bryan, this steady disclosure is presented as the uncomfortable shattering of his belief that he understands Brian–and with that, the possibility that he might build a relationship with him. Tellingly, their first dispute is over Bryan's belief that Brian lied to him about his name, initially calling himself Bill. With that question unresolved, we are left to infer that Brian might be exactly the sort of duplicitous bisexual who passes as gay, but who plans to escape back to a heterosexual life without a trace. At the same time, the film also discloses the extent to which Brian is trapped within a series of assumptions which he has neither invited nor sustained. Bryan deploys a stereotypical gay male's conception of bisexuality–"Let me tell you what is dangerous . . . people hiding behind words like 'bisexual' while thousands of people are dying"–and as he later argues, "It's like you're making me into an object, a hole . . . any opening's going to do for you." His refusal to view bisexuality as anything other than a risk, a closet, a lie, or an indiscriminate appetite, runs up against Brian's confident ability to integrate his sexuality into his life, which in turn exposes the foolishness of Bryan's willingness to make such vitriolic assumptions. Bryan believes that he should have been told, but is forced to recognize that it is he who assumed that Brian was *not* bisexual. He has acted as if he had grounds to know, when in fact he had no reason to believe that he was in a position to characterize Brian's sexuality in advance.

The similarity between these two sorts of knowledge that a gay man might want from a potential sexual partner (are you HIV positive? are you a married bisexual?) draws attention to the ways in which AIDS and bisexuality are both used to address three central questions raised in the film: what does it mean to know the truth about oneself?; under what conditions should that truth be communicated to others?; and who is responsible for the consequences of that transmission? And behind these is an overarching issue: how can one man take into account the most important details about another?

There are thus a series of parallels being made in the film between bisexuality and HIV: how much does Brian know about himself (does he know whether he is gay, straight, or bisexual?/does he know whether or not he is HIV positive?); how much should Brian have told Bryan (should he have disclosed his bisexuality?/should he have disclosed his sexual history?); and should Bryan have made the assumptions that he did in making the choices that he did (should he have assumed that Brian was gay and single when he decided to have sex?/should he have assumed that Brian was HIV negative before having unsafe sex?). Bisexuality and HIV thus both stand as emblems of the unknown truth of a sexual partner, which one overlooks at one's risk and which should not be assumed to be absent concerns in any sexual encounter between men.

We might well want to criticize the conflation–however metaphorical–of bisexuality and HIV, given that bisexual men feature so prominently in conservative discourses about HIV transmission, being seen as irresponsible carriers of HIV from a supposedly self-contained "gay community" to a supposedly defenseless and innocent "straight society." Such critical work has already been done, and done well (see, for instance, Farajajé-Jones, 1995), and will not be the focus of this essay. I am interested rather in the film as a particular instance of such a conflation, which it inflects in ways that are revealing of the consequences of perceiving bisexuality as hidden, undisclosed, and threatening. And I mean this not as an accusation against the film, but rather as a recognition of the legitimacy of using these experiences to speak of one another. For whatever the inappropriateness and risk of the metaphorical folding together of the two, it is still the case that we *do* make metaphors out of our experiences. To hope that AIDS should not become a metaphor out of respect for the seriousness of the crisis is to ignore the ways that the metaphoric potential of all languages and experiences serves as a resource for the mapping out of the meanings by which we make sense of our daily lives. In that sense, the question I want to ask is not: what injustices and prejudices are disclosed through this linkage? But rather: what fears, tensions, and dilemmas within the contemporary experiences of gay and bisexual men is this linkage being made to symbolize?

For this figuring of bisexuality in terms of a dangerous transmission, a life-changing declaration from another that jeopardizes its recipient, runs counter to the film's larger wish to have us share, exchange, transmit, receive. Against its affirmation of the need for men to absorb the offerings that pass between one another, the imaging of bisexuality in terms of HIV transmission enables the film to render the process of sharing secrets to be a dangerous and uncomfortable one. But on what are these fears based? Can we see ways in which the film–and the wider conditions of its possibility–require that it envision this meeting between a gay and a bisexual man as fraught with peril? What is there to be afraid of?

TOGETHER

Let us take in turn each part of the film's title: its affirmation that bisexual and gay men can find ways to be together, its fear that bisexual and gay men will always remain alone. The possibility that they can be together depends primarily on the way in which their differences are posed as a problem. The entire movement of the film is towards a final handshake, in close-up, that passes between them before Brian leaves. If that represents the possibility of a union or understanding between them, it appears as the resolution to all the ways in which they have thus far been unable to meet or reconcile their differences. Togetherness is thus the craving that underlies their failures to find agreement.

Together Alone is particularly insistent in its demarcation of the two men as different. At every possible point, it seeks to separate or differentiate them, and the catalogue of devices the film uses here is itself telling of the assumption that we are two different species of men–a position which I shall suggest raises several serious problems. Emblematic of their differences is a dream that they both have after sex. In their dream, Bryan swims underwater, an environment in which Brian is nervous and distressed; then, when the two grow wings and fly, it is Bryan who is uncomfortable. Their different sexual identities are mapped onto two environments, as if their sexualities assign them to different worlds in which the other can temporarily reside, but to which he cannot belong.

The film's desire to draw distinctions between the two men in the dream is merely one moment in its general desire to depict them as separate. "Opposites attract" reads the cover of my videocassette, a tag spelled out when Bryan insists on showing Brian a yin-yang symbol and explaining its applicability to their situation. The film's delight in such a symbol becomes even more insistent when the figure is clumsily literalized by Bryan's hair being blond and Brian's dark. It is further worked into the narrative by the first distinction made between them; before we have even seen their faces, we see them traveling home in different ways: Bryan cycles back from the bar, while Brian drives.

The financial division hinted at in such a distinction is confirmed when we learn that Brian earned an MBA and works as a marketing director, bearing out Bryan's claim that he "thrived on climbing up the corporate ladder." Bryan's occupation is never disclosed, but his use of the bicycle and the ecological language of many of his narratives suggest that he has no similar interest in being a part of the hierarchies of corporate America. Moreover, Brian's status as an uncouth businessman is played off against Bryan's general knowledge of culture and aesthetics and his learned appearance, which even extends to his wearing reading glasses. Conversely, Brian's academic credentials are restricted to references to his MBA.

Such distinctions are also demarcated along lines of gender. Bryan chooses to be fucked, but Brian only fucks his male partners; Brian's criticisms are rational and assertive, Bryan's waspish and camp; when Brian's narrative of his lost lover reduces him to tears, Bryan holds and comforts him, but when Bryan tells a similarly mournful tale, Brian analyzes it ruthlessly and critically. Even at the level of the physical, the two actors encode stereotypical masculinity and femininity: Brian is taller, broader, has a deeper voice, and his physical strength is emphasized when he beats Bryan at wrestling.

But their differences map them not only through notions of gender (masculine/feminine), but also through those of sexual sensibility, as they lead lives that might be called straight and gay respectively. Brian's heavier identification with mainstream masculinity translates into his incorporation into the rituals, conventions, and limitations of heterosexuality. For example, Brian refers to "the prostrate gland," enabling Bryan to affirm his greater (sub)cultural capital through correcting him. Brian, his character constructed as a stereotypical straight man, is uneducated in the meanings, functions, and politics of his own body; Bryan, constructed as a stereotypical gay man, is not only able to name the organs correctly, but demonstrates confident knowledge of the implications of AIDS for the male body. He is thus also able to offer Brian a lesson in the relative risks of their sexual practices, for, as a figure more ensconced in supposed heterosexual ignorance, Brian is less aware of the risks of HIV transmission in the sex that he has, and it falls to Bryan to explain the dangers and to outline the advantages of testing. Similarly, Brian is made all the more contemptible for a gay audience by lamenting that "you've got these militant drag queens demanding that we all come out of our closets and force ourselves on society," earning a scathing history lesson on the Stonewall riots from Bryan.

This is not to say that Bryan is presented as the model homosexual activist, against whom Brian appears as a shallow bisexual philanderer. For Bryan's particular construction as representative gay man is itself an object of criticism. His camp often appears as an ill-judged mockery of Brian's emotional disclosures, and his "feminized" emotions give him a tendency to respond with sulks, snaps, and barbed comments rather than attempting to hold a conversation. Although his explanations of relative risk and the advantages of testing are very logical, he makes no attempt to listen to Brian's coherent explanation of the reasons behind his own choices. Similarly, he turns the two men's complicated accounts of sexual identity into simplistic political positions whose painful narrowness Brian points out to him. Furthermore, Bryan's characteristic swiftness to find faults leads to the revelation that he is unable to tolerate any relationship for longer than a few months, while Brian has managed to construct an enduring relationship which embraces his bisexuality. And while Brian has been able to integrate his sexuality into his life in a way that affirms his desire, Bryan nervously admits that he has been too afraid to have sex for several years.

Thus if Brian's connection to heterosexual masculinity leaves him aggressive, cold, bullying, and ignorant, Bryan's ties to gay culture leave him judgmental, over-sensitive, unable to recognize sexual fluidity, keener to sloganize than to empathize, and prone to quoting Emily Dickinson. All of which might suggest that gay men can find as much to be offended by in the film as bi men.

And yet the point of these marked differences is not to ridicule each individual or their wider communities, but to affirm the possibility and the necessity of finding workable relationships across these differences. However, in order to conceive of the necessity of reconciliation, the film must first assume the inevitability of our separation. Even as we, as gay and bisexual men, speak of the need for or the desirability of closer participation and cooperation, we invoke and assume our non-connection–a problem which I do not feel that I have solved for myself in writing this essay. The film's utopian dream of reconciliation, however laudable, thus requires that the two men be different: feminine/masculine; gay community/straight community; fair/dark; well informed/poorly informed.

It may thus be that in attempting to negotiate between our (imagined or assumed) differences, we–like *Together Alone*–risk erasing our similarities. The rigidity of the film's demarcation between the two men forecloses the possibility that we may not be so fixedly different. I am thinking here not only of the general point that stereotyping reduces the diversity of experience that it purports to represent, but also of the deeper assumptions that underlie these divisions.

First, the division of the two into representatives of radically opposed forms of identity erases the possibility of an autonomous and articulate bisexual politics. Since bisexuality is seen as railing against the limitations of identity politics, it thus appears not to be in itself a theoretical critique so much as a wail of individualism. Yet the specificity of bisexual male experience is not only, as it is for this film, that of refusing the labels of rigidly monosexist cultures, but also that of inhabiting a bisexual culture with its own coherence. For Brian, bisexuality has no culture, no rituals, no meeting places, no community for itself–it only takes place in spaces that belong to others. Against which, I would suggest that one key issue for gay and bisexual men is how we can learn from one another's experiences as we construct distinct communities that nevertheless intersect and overlap.

Second, their separateness circumvents any recognition that what appears to divide the two men may not in fact be a permanent mark of difference. In valorizing the truth of disclosure, the film sides with a more rigid notion of identity than it otherwise appears to endorse. It would seem to assert that, finally, Bryan is gay, but can accept Brian's understanding of what it means for him to be bi; Brian is bi, but can accept Bryan's understanding of what it means for him to be gay. What is missing from such a reconciliation is the recognition that neither of those sexual identities is itself fixed and that each might contain or become the other. It is not simply the case that "gay" and "bisexual" are separate entities whose distinctness is in the interests of both communities. Rather, at various points bisexual men may redefine their identities and desires as gay, and gay men may redefine theirs as bisexual. We cross and recross these borders, which does not cause them to cease to exist, but which should demand that we reconceptualize what sorts of borders they are.

Third, it is worth commenting on the status of women within the film. Both men refer to women in their lives and laugh together when Bryan relates a misogynistic story about his female psychiatrist:

> Bryan: I stopped seeing her though when she told me I had vagina envy.

> Brian: A lesbian, no doubt.

> Bryan: No, just a political post-Freudian neo-feminist. She committed suicide a few years later when she set her bra on fire when she was wearing it.

Given the apparent absence of any irony in this exchange, perhaps what bisexual and gay men need to address collectively is our relative male privilege in a patriarchal world. In the light of such concerns, I would suggest that what defines the relationship between gay and bisexual men are not our differences, but rather that we are similar in ways that the film does not know how to begin to articulate.

Yet, in a sense, it is the very rigidity of the distinctions and stereotypes which the film deploys which invites the audience to go beyond them. The care with which the two are constructed as dissimilar itself acts as a kind of alienation effect, inviting us not to take its narrative as representative of any real differences. Rather, it may be that through its insistent simplification, we are encouraged to ask what other sorts of differences may apply in gay/bi encounters and to what extent they are touched by similar problems.

Such a reading suggests that there may be some efficacy in the use of stereotypes within texts, since, as in this case, they may serve to distance a film from authenticity, thereby encouraging us not to see its particular forms of bisexuality and gayness as necessarily aspiring to an accuracy which is, after all, always impossible to achieve. Moreover, as Grover (1991) has pointed out, it is unfair to condemn material that personally jars with our notion of how we would want our communities represented, simply because there is a scarcity of images to represent them. Grover argues that as sexual dissidents, we overinvest in the limited number of images that we do have, whereas those whose identities are routinely represented in a greater variety of ways are less likely to feel personally attacked by images that do not reflect their own values.

On the other hand, whatever the merits of the unconventional and creative deployment and reading of stereotypes, we should remember that the meanings given to a film are determined by the contexts which pre-exist it. For example, even though the film meticulously gives equal priority to its two characters and their divergent sexualities, the BFI's CD-ROM Film Index describes *Together Alone* as: "About Bryan, a young gay man who feels insecure because of the AIDS epidemic, and his relationship with a man with whom he spends the night." Brian has no name or attributes; he is simply a character in Bryan's story. It may not be enough for a film to be equally scrupulous about the visibility of gay and bisexual men when the context within which such scrupulousness will be situated is one that is already pre-disposed to grant gay men greater visibility.[2]

ALONE

At the end of the film, Brian and Bryan are not *together.* Brian says he would like to meet again (but he may be lying) and leaves the name of his hotel (which may be false); Bryan promises to call (and he too may be lying). The extent of their differences makes them uneasy and is a pertinent reminder that the work of making connections is not comfortable. That the film ends with their parting is then the final comment on the impossibility of any simple reconciliation of these differences. This mode of being together involves not unification, elision of differences, or discovery of shared identity, but the mutual acceptance of absolute incompatibility. If the politics of their mutual liberal acceptance is that each has the right to be as he is, this necessitates the film's conviction that such a situation leaves each one of them *alone.*

The recurrent concern for both characters that their perceptions and interpretations remain inviolate and receive respect is, of course, symptomatic of the existential dilemmas of what some of us call modernity, some late modernity, and some postmodernity. Hall and Neitz (1993) propose that modern subjectivity is organized around a mode of individualism in which the central value is the affirmation of one's own unique emotional vantage point on life, codified as a set of opinions and feelings about politics, relationships, morality, aesthetics, and so on. However, since any set of values is held to be subjective and thereby authentic, the affirmation of one's own point of view faces a particular problem: it is precisely its subjective status that assures its authenticity, since it is thereby proven to be one's own individual and original perspective. Hence, through its very subjectivity, it becomes an obstacle to finding a way of sharing values and tastes with others. Although the subjective expression of one's own perspective is an affirmation of identity, it is not one that can be readily affirmed by others, since it is precisely its not being shared by our interlocutors that guarantees its authenticity.

Such an account is essentially a version of the traditionally modern malady of anomie, which in *Together Alone* is figured as the impossibility of finding a shared set of interpretations, an impossibility that as a culture we in fact find necessary and desirable, since without difference we cannot have the sense of autonomous selfhood that we have come to feel that we need. "I'm not quite sure I see things the way you do," Bryan announces, and it is around that notion of individualistic selfhood that the conflict centers. It is to their own individual needs that each appeals as grounds for the other's actions: Bryan's final appeal for a disclosure of HIV status from Brian is that "I'd like you to tell me for my own personal satisfaction." Similarly, it is to the distinctiveness of his point of view that each appeals in order to escape criticism. For example, Brian justifies his decision not to take an HIV test on the grounds that "I know me, I know myself, and I know I couldn't deal with it."

Each character is thus "alone" in the sense that the other inhabits a different world from him. Indeed, Brian is literally only in town for a few days, with his place of origin never given. Between the two lies not a simple gulf of difference, but a gulf resulting from the necessity of non-coincidence that is distinctively modern. Giddens (1990) suggests that modernity is marked by a loss of trust in those around us that results from the erosion of shared geographies, values, and skills. We can no longer be sure of what another believes, or of the grounds for believing that we know them, since modernity has replaced a world founded on security with one based on uncertainty. Communal values dissolve into a variety of specialized individualistic ethical codes (53-54); pools of shared knowledge are replaced with a diversity of professional specialties nearly incomprehensible to those outside of them (27-28); and local communities are transformed into open spaces traversed by non-inhabitants (101-03). Indeed, according to Giddens, what most defines the experience inaugurated by the Enlightenment is that anything which has so far been true, may yet be discredited (48-49).

Such an environment of constant uncertainty appears in the film in the form of the opacity of each man to the guesses of the other: their respective assumptions about each other constantly prove mistaken. For instance, whenever each recounts an event from his life, the other attempts to second-guess how the story will end, only to be proven wrong. When Bryan tells of his most intense relationship with another man, Brian mistakenly assumes that it is a sexual relationship, only to have it pointed out to him that it was platonic; when Brian tells the story of the person who most hurt him, Bryan assumes that it is a man and has to be corrected about the gender. Within such an individualist notion of selfhood, there is thus no way of generalizing from one's own sexual history about the sexual histories of others. *Together Alone* insists on the impossibility of finding secure vantage points from which to buttress oneself against the surprise of what we do not yet know about others. Its stress on Bryan's faith that his gay identity guarantees a secure understanding of the world suggests then that identity politics is at least partly a defense against such uncertainty. Yet what the film ultimately dramatizes is the failure of such confidence; however coherent and elaborate the network of assumptions about male behavior that affix to the notion of "gay," they are not able to encompass, explain, or predict the diversity of male behaviors that in fact exist.

This suggests the importance of the film's dialogic structure. On the one hand, it might appear to be governed by notions of the inner truth of the human subject: are you or are you not HIV positive?; are you or are you not bisexual? In its gradual revealing of increasingly intimate "truths" about its characters, the film would seem to suggest that there is such a constant and meaningful core to be accessed within each of us. We may well imagine that such dialogue searches for closure, for that final judgment which reaches and names the truth of the other about whom it speaks. In such a reading, it would follow the logic that Barthes (1990: 208) sees behind the lovers' quarrel: the desire to finish a row by having the last word.

Yet, on the other hand, this is also the mode of dialogue most typically used by soap operas, and which functions there to extend the uncertainty about which character's account or explanation is true. For soaps, the joyfully interminable dialogue keeps the audience's interest precisely by holding off the interpretation of any one character over another. Of this form of accusation and counter-accusation, interpretation and counter-interpretation, Ang has remarked that "the status of the spoken word is therefore relativized" (1985: 73). In the world of competing claims, there is not so much an assertion of the possibility of final knowledge, as there is its impossibility.

Thus even as the film hopes for a disclosure of truth, it also militates heavily against it. For even the disclosure of key events should be read not as the revealing of truth, but as one way of telling a life-story so that it works to define the sort of identity that makes most sense in this particular location. As Simon (1996: 30) notes of sexual histories, their contents, meanings, and the interpretations put on them will vary depending on the motives for any given telling.

Consequently, insofar as Brian and Bryan find a way to be *together*, it is not because they come to know and understand each other, so much as because they come to know that they can never finally know or understand each other. Their interpretations do not bring them closer to a given truth, but only underscore the absolute relativity of their viewpoints, which is necessary, since, as we have seen, each is conceived as radically different from the other. So even as the film is driven by the desire to have the last word, it dramatizes the possibility that pleasure, communication, and forming a relationship only come into being by the impossibility of this–by the undercutting of attempts to have the last word. In the forms of connection that we make across our differences, it may not be that we fix our differences, so much as that we are able to recognize their provisionality insofar as we put them into question once we start the process of defining, modifying, revising, and negotiating their meanings with another.

Such a mode of linking together our various alone-nesses has been commented on by Phelan (1994). She insists that the process of making connections is not simply one that adds together existing discrete attributes, but rather is one in which we become transformed through newly imagined future possibilities. Thus she proposes that: "The problem for coalition politics is not 'What do we share?' but rather 'What might we share as we develop our identities through a process of coalition?'" (1994: 140). Therefore, in making and building upon connections, we make for ourselves new identities, values, and goals which did not preexist the coalition, and could not preexist it, since it was itself the necessary precondition for their conception.

Yet even as it opens up such possibilities for forms of becoming that we do not yet know we may be capable of, *Together Alone* also seeks to establish solidity of meaning in an altogether less promising way. Faced with the problems caused by the differences separating the characters, the film attempts to reunite them by finding a discourse which both characters can adhere to: one of popular morality and pop-psychology. Here, responsibility, openness, love, and courage are the keywords for defining what is good and healthy, while shame, secrecy, fear, and irresponsibility define what is unacceptable or neurotic. Such values surface in the form of pithy, compact phrases common to a popular therapeutic discourse: "Maybe you're afraid to get close to anybody"; "You have to try and work things out, not run away"; "You've got to hope for something better, you've got to hope for tomorrow." The solution to the aloneness of modernity is thus the togetherness of cliché. The film's method of staging agreement is to invoke a series of clichés which then act as the "universal solvent" which enables differences to be eroded and a meeting place to be found.

Indeed, in attempting both to ward off and to respond to the charges of cliché that the script seems to invite, Bryan declares, "At the risk of sounding like a total fool and a complete cliché [a phrase that has become itself already a cliché?], I've never met anyone like you."

Becoming cliché is less the risk of Bryan's declaration of his feelings, than it is of the film's entire search for a way of finding familiarity between the men. Indeed, if the function of his line is to affirm that experiences which take the form of clichés are nevertheless habitable and important, I would go further and suggest that, for this film, cliché is the only mode through which shared values become possible at all.

Such a situation should be of some concern for bisexual activists, since it is this very desire to bridge difference that is the focus of so much of our energy–and just like *Together Alone,* some of our most popular rallying documents take the form of clichés which seek to make connections between these differences. For instance, however important June Jordan's "A New Politics of Sexuality" has been for affirming the legitimacy of bisexual political possibility, I am still nagged with doubt when I read a claim such as: "What tyranny could exceed a tyranny that dictates to the human heart, and that attempts to dictate the public career of an honest human body?" (1996: 13).

I am not convinced that my body is the source of honesty; it seems to me to be equally a deceptive object, which would rather stay in bed and eat chocolate than contribute to hard political campaigns, and whose desires are often reactionary and repressive. I am not convinced that the alliterated human heart is the origin of the most progressive intentions–the human heart seems to me to be equally capable of specious sentimentality, arrogant posturing, and naive religious fervor. I dislike the way that the freedoms of the sexual body are eclipsing the freedoms of the laboring body, so that we feel that gay men should be glad to work in gay bars where they can be out, rather than asking whether or not their bosses pay them a decent wage.

Yet the rhetoric of cliché does appeal to us–as it does to any struggling political movement–and it does so, I am suggesting, because as with Brian and Bryan's attempts to find a common ground, it is a discourse which we are willing to take for granted. It appears to subdue difference under words that we all feel that we can agree with. It is not difficult to get the bisexual movement to assent to the freedom of the human heart. But it might be more productive to think about getting the bisexual movement to assent to a decent minimum wage or just immigration laws. If ideals unite, then policies divide–hence our

tendency to steer clear of them in favor of egalitarian pronounce-
ments.[3]

Such a suspicion of the magic of cliché is not to deny its effectivity
or its appeal; I chose to write about *Together Alone* because it still fills
me with faith that even in the face of the sorts of hostility that it
explores, there are ways for gay and bisexual men to speak with each
other. Yet, while the film makes me feel that gay and bisexual men
need not be alone, it makes it no clearer to me how we are to resolve
the more substantial gulfs between us. To the extent that cliché pre-
tends to offer us a mode of unity, it does so only by silencing a
discussion of the differences that threaten to shatter that apparent
harmony and to return us to our alone-ness.

How, as bisexual men, are we to speak of the pleasure of women's
bodies in the face of what a gay man once described to me as
"chopped liver syndrome": the widespread disgust amongst gay men
at the female body? In what ways can those bisexual men who have
little or no cultural recognition of the institutional realities of homophobia contribute to the struggles of gay men? What role is there for
those bisexual men who argue that it is their right to express male-fe-
male sexual pleasure in spaces carved out for the affirmation of same-
sex desire? In what ways can bisexual organizations affirm a place for
the gay male partners of bisexual men, rather than assuming that such
"monosexual" partners pose some sort of a problem?

It may be inappropriate to expect our art to answer these questions–
and it is certainly the case that activists are making important headway
on all of them. But what bisexual and gay men need are not clichés
that affirm the essential similarity of our experiences–a solution to our
being alone–so much as attention to the material spaces which will
generate shared practical concerns, perhaps as yet unimagined, and
out of which come projects that forge connections across these differences.

DISPUTATIONS

I began this essay by asking why the unknowability of another
man's HIV status might be taken up as a metaphor for the unknowabil-

ity of his sexuality. I have suggested that in the case of *Together Alone* there are three reasons. Firstly, the film suggests that the unknowability of the men that we meet impedes the possibilities that we can form relationships with them in ways that make us feel comfortable or secure. Secondly, it suggests that to receive unexpected knowledge about the inner life of a sexual partner is itself transformative: just as Bryan might be transformed by infection, so too is he transformed by the new perspectives that Brian challenges him to respond to. Finally, it suggests that insofar as we meet only through finding a shared language of mutually satisfying assumptions, we can live with what we receive from another man only by finding a framework in which to locate it. In all these ways, AIDS is taken up by the film as a serviceable metaphor for what it takes to be the value of knowing, the risk of knowing, and the possibility of transforming uncertainty into certainty.

I have also suggested that I find all of these positions unsatisfying–and it might seem that there is something willfully perverse in my approach to this film. When it urges that we are all different, I criticize it on the grounds that in fact there are similarities between us that are being occluded. When it says that we are similar, I criticize it on the grounds that it is overlooking our differences. And yet it is in my particular desire to pick a fight with the film that I find the text fascinating. For it is in my antagonistic, resentful interrogation of it that the conflicts that it represents take on a new level of meaning. Are they not the mirror of my own reactions as a reader? Just as Bryan misreads Brian, and Brian mistreats Bryan, I feel compelled to criticize, mistreat, and misjudge *Together Alone*–I feel insulted by it, and its makers might well feel insulted by me. Yet, as the film itself stresses, it is out of our disagreements, mutual antipathies, and failures to agree that the liveliness of engaging takes place. I could say of the film, as Brian says, "you have to admit there is a certain something between us." To which Bryan replies: "Animosity?"

And it is in this affirmation of the politics of animosity that I find the text most hopeful. Not so much in its assertion that we can solve our differences (for I see no reason to assume that we can); not in the claim that we are essentially similar (for I do not believe that similarity entails affection); nor in its faith that we must always hope for a better tomorrow (which history would seem to belie). Rather, my hope is in the film's willingness to affirm the necessity–or even the pleasure–of extended exchanges of petty intolerances, supercilious judgments, arrogant claims, self-deceiving confidences, narcissistic autobiographical narratives, narrow-minded interpretations, and ingrained hostilities. The final aesthetic achievement of the film is that it makes a watchable spectacle out of what passes between us when we do not get along, and its correlative political achievement is to insist that there is a usefulness in those sorts of embittered and painful rows.

And so I return to Mark White. Perhaps what interests me about him is precisely the recognition that here is the most unlikely of points at which to start building an alliance. Here indeed is a level of acrimony which would seem to foreclose the notion of "alliance" before it has even begun. But it is this animosity that begs the notion of a view of politics which goes beyond the recognized necessity of shared spaces, political campaigns, support groups, and affirming alliances, and asks us to recognize the value of antagonistic discursive spaces, in which we air our dirty laundry publicly, bitterly, without any intention of supporting each other.

Notions such as "community" define the modern political landscape as a response to the loss of those forms of religious and geographical solidarity whose demise has so benefited sexual dissidents. The work that communities perform is precisely the imagining of a place of reconciliation, unity, and togetherness-in-difference which the film struggles to articulate. Yet our personal experience of communities suggests much more fluid and volatile entities than that. At times, my connection to the bisexual community has been that of someone who convened a local bisexual group, planned conferences, facilitated workshops, ran "bi awareness trainings" for gay and straight organizations, and edited the U.K. bisexual newsletter. I was "in community" in the sense of constantly talking with, meeting, e-mailing, and producing with other bisexuals in similar situations. Now I am related to the bisexual community insofar as I might refer to it in an undergraduate lecture on identities, or because I write a letter of complaint to the magazine that runs Mark White's article, or because I give an interview to a journalist wanting to rebut it.[4] I am part of the bisexual community insofar as there are two other bisexuals in my shared house, or because my lovers, and their lovers, are also bisexual, even though we do not, by and large, have that kind of face-to-face participation in the movement.

To describe such participation in the community is to refigure the boundaries of that community, the notions of where its spaces extend to, the catalogue of points that comprise it, and the forms of language that embody it. Do I, for instance, become a member of the U.S. bisexual community through contributing to this volume? We must extend community to encompass spaces, relationships, and sites of discourse that do not belong comfortably within a more restrictive notion of the community of togetherness. And, in doing so, I suggest that the film invites us to rethink the meanings of friction and discomfort. Rather than assuming that differences mark the limit of a community, I am suggesting that, in practice, communities need not simply bring together people who are like us, or with whom we agree, but can also serve as productive, necessary, and unpleasant links between people who do not get along.

In that sense, the seemingly most useful response to writing like White's would be to resituate the relationship between his account, my letter, and this article. They are themselves part of the terrain of a bisexual community which is not simply a network of those who affirm one another in their bisexuality, but rather an extensive network of places where bisexuality is enunciated and practiced. Such a community is a dispersed trail of bisexual possibilities, which makes bisexuality more varied, more important, and harder to pin down, and which also demands that we think of "community" as residing in the exchanges which fail to provide, or even which actively inhibit, agreement. "The bisexual community" is not those of us who know and are affiliated with the network of organizations listed in *The Bisexual Resource Guide*, or even the expanse of people who are attracted to both women and men but who may not identify themselves as "bisexual." Instead, it is the maze of openings onto possible speculations of bisexuality.

So rather than thinking of the best ways to strengthen "our" community, or even the best ways to strengthen links between communities, the film leads me to think about those provisional contact points that Probyn (1997) calls "outside belongings": forms of connection in which bisexuality is kept alive, put into circulation, provoked, or disputed–and thus becomes more real within the society that circulates it even when that circulation is hostile, since such opportunities may yet be taken up by bisexual voices and spoken of in new ways. I am interested in the fact that, however bisexuality is named, interpreted, or enunciated, I remain free to respond to it in creative ways–so that bisexual possibilities are kept in lively motion even through those cultural clashes that most enrage us.

To end then with one final disputation with *Together Alone*: I am dissatisfied that it takes place in the private world of the bedroom. That in itself seems to me to be an attempt to avoid the possibility that these are rows that need to occur in public. It seems to say that this discomfort is something which we must suffer in private, so that we may forge a politically necessary united front. The film's vision of a dialogue between gay and bisexual men is thus one in which unity and solidarity remain the watchwords of the day in the political arena.

And then, conversely, to end with an affirmation of its value: by staging this petty bickering as an object for mass consumption, *Together Alone* undoes that logic by arguing instead that we need to talk about these things in the bar afterwards, on the bus on the way home, with our friends, and at our conferences. Its vision of a dialogue between gay and bisexual men is thus one in which uncomfortable voices speak all around us, and in which a dispersed community develops through their conflicts.

NOTES

1. *Attitude* is a glossy magazine aimed primarily, although by no means exclusively, at gay men and is available through conventional highstreet retailers. Its aim is to feed aspects of gay culture across into mainstream contexts. Although this article's views on bisexuality are representative of certain tensions between gay and bisexual men, a more recent issue carried an article arguing that a bisexual "floodgate" had opened, and concluding: "Sexual/gender identity is on the move for everyone. We're here, maybe we're a little bit queer, better get used to it" (Olley, 1999).

2. Similarly, whatever the care with which the film dissects Bryan's bigotry, a bisexual reviewer can still write that the director "manages to reinforce every existing negative stereotype about bisexual men" (Bryant, 1997: 76), as if the film

endorses Bryan's sentiments rather than so obviously deriding them. For an assessment of the range of ways available for reading bisexual images, see Bi Academic Intervention (1997).

3. These are not, of course, areas that Jordan's own wider work overlooks. Rather, my concern is with the ways in which this rhetoric lends itself to being embraced by a bisexual politics which is not itself necessarily interested in such issues.

4. In due course, I wrote an outraged letter to the editor. It didn't get published, but I was later contacted by a journalist from Britain's altogether more down to earth *Gay Times* who was writing a pointed rebuttal of White's position. Simon Birch, "It's What I Am," *Gay Times,* January 1998: 38-40.

REFERENCES

Ang, Ien. 1985. *Watching Dallas: Soap Opera and the Melodramatic Imagination.* London: Methuen.

Barthes, Roland. 1990. *A Lover's Discourse: Fragments,* trans. Richard Howard. New York: Noonday Press.

Bi Academic Intervention, ed. 1997. *The Bisexual Imaginary: Representation, Identity and Desire.* London: Cassell.

Bryant, Wayne M. 1997. *Bisexual Characters in Film: From Anaïs to Zee.* Binghamton, NY: Harrington Park Press.

Cagle, Chris. 1996. Rough Trade: Sexual Taxonomy in Postwar America. In *RePresenting Bisexualities: Subjects and Cultures of Fluid Desire,* eds. Donald E. Hall and Maria Pramaggiore, 234-52. New York: New York University Press.

Donaldson, Stephen. 1995. The Bisexual Movement's Beginnings in the 70s: A Personal Retrospective. In *Bisexual Politics: Theories, Queries, and Visions,* ed. Naomi Tucker, 31-45. Binghamton, NY: Harrington Park Press.

Farajajé-Jones, Elias. 1995. Fluid Desire: Race, HIV/AIDS, and Bisexual Politics. In *Bisexual Politics: Theories, Queries, and Visions,* ed. Naomi Tucker, 119-30. Binghamton, NY: Harrington Park Press.

Giddens, Anthony. 1990. *The Consequences of Modernity.* Cambridge: Polity Press.

Grover, Jan Zita. 1990. Framing the Questions: Positive Imaging and Scarcity in Lesbian Photographs. In *Stolen Glances: Lesbians Take Photographs,* eds. Tessa Boffin and Jean Fraser, 184-90. London: Pandora Press.

Jordan, June. 1996. A New Politics of Sexuality. In *Bisexual Horizons: Politics, Histories, Lives,* eds. Sharon Rose, Cris Stevens, et al., 11-15. London: Lawrence and Wishart.

Olley, Michelle. 1999. Children of the Revolution. *Attitude* (January): 70-74.

Phelan, Shane. 1994. *Getting Specific: Postmodern Lesbian Politics.* Minneapolis: University of Minnesota Press.

Power, Lisa. 1996. Forbidden Fruit. In *Anti-Gay,* ed. Mark Simpson, 55-64. London: Cassell.

Probyn, Elspeth. 1996. *Outside Belongings.* London: Routledge.

Simon, William. 1996. *Postmodern Sexualities.* London: Routledge.

Udis-Kessler, Amanda. 1995. Identity/Politics: A History of the Bisexual Movement. In *Bisexual Politics: Theories, Queries, and Visions,* ed. Naomi Tucker, 17-30. Binghamton, NY: Harrington Park Press.

Bisexual Dilemma:

Closets all the way down

© 2002 by The Haworth Press, Inc. All rights reserved.

[Haworth co-indexing entry note]: "Bisexual Dilemma: Closets All the Way Down." Clurman, Dan. Co-published simultaneously in *Journal of Bisexuality* (Harrington Park Press, an imprint of The Haworth Press, Inc.) Vol. 2, No. 1, 2002, p. 37; and: *Bisexual Men in Culture and Society* (ed: Brett Beemyn and Erich Steinman) Harrington Park Press, an imprint of The Haworth Press, Inc., 2002, p. 37. Single or multiple copies of this article are available for a fee from The Haworth Document Delivery Service [1-800-342-9678, 9:00 a.m. - 5:00 p.m. (EST). E-mail address: getinfo@haworthpressinc.com].

Bisexuals Who Kill

Hollywood's Bisexual Crimewave, 1985-1998

Jonathan David White

© 2002 by The Haworth Press, Inc. All rights reserved.

[Haworth co-indexing entry note]: "Bisexuals Who Kill: Hollywood's Bisexual Crimewave, 1985-1998." White, Jonathan David. Co-published simultaneously in *Journal of Bisexuality* (Harringtor Park Press, an imprint of The Haworth Press, Inc.) Vol. 2, No. 1, 2002, pp. 39-54; and: *Bisexual Men in Culture and Society* (ed: Brett Beemyn and Erich Steinman) Harrington Park Press, an imprint of The Haworth Press, Inc., 2002, pp. 39-54. Single or multiple copies of this article are available for a fee from The Haworth Document Delivery Service [1-800-342-9678, 9:00 a.m. - 5:00 p.m. (EST). E-mail address: getinfo@ haworthpressinc.com].

SUMMARY. In a number of Hollywood films from 1985-1995, bisexual characters were represented as violent, drug-using murderers. With relatively few representations of bisexual men and women in mainstream cinema during this period, the near-uniformity with which such films as *Basic Instinct, Blue Velvet, American Commandos,* and *Chained Heat II* depicted bisexuals as killers suggests that a deeper ideological substitution was taking place. Tracing the particular history of this trope, this article finds that media constructions of bisexual men as vectors of HIV transmission in the mid-1980s played a decisive role in creating the image of the bisexual man as sexualized killer. This figure fused representations of unrestrained heterosexual-patriarchal power with queer subversion, as epitomized in *Blue Velvet.* In turn, in the early 1990s, these images were transposed onto bisexual women, most influentially in *Basic Instinct,* to form a new category of heterosexist representation modeled after depictions of bisexual men, rather than traditional images of lesbians. The construction of bisexual identity as a form of sadomasochistic, drug-linked criminality served as a public appeal for greater state repression of bisexual communities. *[Article copies available for a fee from The Haworth Document Delivery Service: 1-800-342-9678. E-mail address: <getinfo@haworthpressinc.com> Website: <http://www. HaworthPress.com> © 2002 by The Haworth Press, Inc. All rights reserved.]*

KEYWORDS. *Basic Instinct,* bisexual men, bisexuality, *Blue Velvet,* crime, drugs, film, violence

According to Hollywood, our country is in the throes of a drug-related bisexual crimewave. Recent popular film confronts us with a new mythology of terror and suspicion, set in a world of ice-pick murders, dismemberments, rapes, and torture, and populated by junkies, coke-crazed psychos, SM gangsters, and slut butchers: the underworld of bisexuals who kill. This crisis for law and order began in the mid-1980s in films that portrayed bisexual men as nemeses, such as *Mike's Murder* (1984), *American Commandos* (1985), and *Blue Velvet* (1986). By the early 1990s, however, the threat to public safety and morality had been extended to include bisexual women, with movies like *Basic Instinct* (1992), *Chained Heat II* (1993), *Showgirls* (1995), and the remake of Henri-Georges Clouzot's *Diabolique* (1996). Looking at such images can help a great deal in understanding how bisexual men and women have been constructed in U.S. popular culture, the interrelatedness of these constructions, and the relationship between the images of bisexuals in the dominant media and in queer political activism. Hollywood's creation of a bi crimewave might also offer some insights into the larger question of bisexuality's place in the sexual political economy of the contemporary United States. For example, the cinematic killing spree may help to explain the peculiar visibility of bisexual men in popular culture in the mid- and late 1980s, and the subsequent near-total disappearance of the figure of the bi man, to be replaced by the equally stereotyped and ideologized bi woman. It may also help to explain why the popular cultural discourses used to describe bi women in the 1990s relate more to the model developed to characterize bisexual men than to traditional representations of lesbians.

In *American Commandos* (1985), the straight, white Vietnam vet hero searches for the white and Latino junkies who have murdered his young son, raped his Asian American wife, and driven her to commit suicide (with a knife, in classically racist Madame Butterfly style). His investigation leads him to a seedy, lightless bar–an "AC/DC joint" in the words of his informant–where, among other sordid bisexuals, he finds and kills the heroin-addicted bisexual man who principally perpetrated the vicious attacks. This image of the male bisexual rapist draws its symbolic power from the double association with HIV: junkie and bisexual man. The bi male rapist fuses male heterosexual power (rapist) and queer positionality (being "AC/DC"), thereby invoking one of the principal forms of biphobia used to counter the growing visibility of bisexual-identified people in the mid-1980s. Male bisexuality is the dangerous eruption of homosexuality within the heterosexual matrix, the sign of the vulnerability of the "straight" world to queers (or, indeed, to *queerness*). As both a bisexual man and an IV drug abuser–two of the figures who, according to the Centers for Disease Control and Prevention (CDC), are "responsible" for "heterosexual AIDS"–the AC/DC junkie rapist is an invasive, alien threat to heterosexual society. He does not merely threaten to transmit AIDS, but in the logic of *American Commandos,* he *is* AIDS. Of course, HIV and bisexuality are profoundly linked politically; the idea that there was a distinct category of bisexual individuals was brought to U.S.

popular attention by repeated news reports which identified "homo-sexual and bisexual men" as high-risk groups for AIDS.

Michael du Plessis reminds us that there is no single "bisexuality," but rather that certain models of bisexuality have currency at particular times and in particular situations. Thus analyses of bisexual identity must begin with an examination of "the ways in which various bisexu-alities have been constructed, interpreted, or excluded" in specific historical conjunctures.[1] In the case of the Hollywood convention of the bisexual male killer, its emergence is rooted in the association of "bisexual men" with AIDS in the dominant social and political dis-courses of the mid-1980s and in the conflation of a number of readily available images of abjection: drug kingpin, serial killer, SM practi-tioner, sex deviant, and gender outlaw. This iconography of human evil has the effect of eliciting both biphobia and calls for that evil to be contained through socially permissible (and often state-sponsored) violence.

The first connection in film between bisexual men and the use and sale of illegal drugs occurs in James Bridges's *Mike's Murder* (1984). In this film, Debra Winger's exploration of the seamy underworld in which her murdered boyfriend moved discloses that he was not only a drug dealer, but also sexually involved with men. This link between male bisexuality, drugs, and murder would become central to the representation of bisexuals in Hollywood for the rest of the decade. In 1985, the year in which CDC Investigator James I. Slaff's *The AIDS Epidemic* blamed bisexual men for "heterosexual AIDS,"[2] and when pie charts of "high risk groups" were common in mainstream news media coverage of HIV, movies like *American Commandos* pro-claimed that it was time to use deadly force to protect "the general population"–a term always used as a code for heterosexual, non-drug-using whites[3]–from the deadly threat of the bisexual intravenous drug user.

By 1986, Hollywood had launched a full-fledged, drug-related bi-sexual crimewave through a variety of movies–not just in exploitation pictures like *American Commandos*. For example, such a quintessen-tial U.S. film of the 1980s as David Lynch's *Blue Velvet* (1986) is also deeply involved in the politics of the "bi peril." As Fredric Jameson points out, the figure of Frank Booth (Dennis Hopper) enables Lynch to interrelate the transgressive images of drugs and sadomasochism.[4] Frank is involved in a murderous drug underworld and is a psychopathic sexual sadist who exploits Dorothy Vallens (Isabella Rossellini). Bisexuality is the crucial third term left out of Jameson's reading of the role of drugs and SM[5] in Frank's character. Male bisexual desire, fused with drugs and sadomasochism, constitute the "evil in the world" that Jeffrey Bellmont (Kyle MacLachlan) discovers when he descends into the seedy nightworld embodied by Frank.

Jameson's strange failure to read Frank as bisexual is itself an interesting illustration of the process whereby homicidal bisexual plots like *Blue Velvet* manifest the simultaneous overdeterminations of hyper-visibility and invisibility. In *Blue Velvet,* as in nearly every movie about bisexuals who kill, the words "bi" and "bisexual" are never uttered.[6] Instead, there is a proliferation of verbal and visual codes and terms related to the idea of bisexuality–and, more particularly, to a given set of biphobic conceptions. This process at once grounds the concept of bisexuality in the readily available stereotypes of the "AC/DC" and the sissified rapist, while simultaneously isolating that self-contained symbolic system from other potential discourses related to the sign "bisexual." This process is particularly significant in light of Maria Pramaggiore's discussion of the complexities involved in recognizing bisexuality in film.[7] Absent the moment in which the Frank Booth character explicitly claims a bisexual identity, a network of power relations and systems of signification regulate the possibilities for recognizing or not recognizing him as bisexual. The cultures of recognition into which *Blue Velvet* seeks to initiate audiences are diametrically opposed politically to the emancipatory possibilities of bisexual spectatorship that Pramaggiore explores; the violent spectacle of Frank's bisexuality, and the silence/invisibility of bisexuality attendant the refusal to use the word, combine to create a system in which viewers (regardless of sexual identity) can only recognize bisexuality in terms of the overdetermined symbolic vocabulary of ritualized biphobia.

Frank's bisexuality, and the menace it represents, first emerge in Frank's interactions with Ben and then in his beating of Jeffrey. Frank flirts with and seduces Ben with a charm very different from the furious orders he gives to his henchmen Raymond (Brad Dourif) and Paul (Jack Nance), his "sexual slave" Dorothy, or the "good neighbor" Jeffrey. Ben (brilliantly played by Dean Stockwell) is the menacing queen *par excellence,* a foppishly dressed man with a long cigarette holder, white painted face, Marilyn Monroe beauty mark, and heavy crimson lipstick, who minces and rolls his eyes in stereotypically gay male ways. Dean Stockwell's casting alludes to his famous performance as another swishing sociopath, Judd Steiner in *Compulsion,* Richard Fleischer's 1959 treatment of the 1924 Leopold-Loeb murder case; certainly Dennis Hopper's Frank has some kinship to the violent Artie Straus (Bradford Dilman), Steiner's lover from *Compulsion.*[8] Like "The Blue Lady," Frank's fantasy projection of Dorothy, Ben is a singer lip-synching to Roy Orbison's "In Dreams," a song that moves Frank like no other except "Blue Velvet." Frank shows off Jeffrey to Ben, boasting, in flirtatiously suggestive tones, "I can make him do whatever I want." For Ben, the brutal queen, this turns into an opportunity to stroke and then punch Jeffrey. Before laughingly disappearing from Ben's living room in an apparent manifestation of his demonic powers, Frank bellows the words that probably most embody the heterosexist terror of bisexuality: "Let's fuck! I'll fuck *anything that moves!*"

After their drive in the country, Frank warns Jeffrey, "Don't you fucking look at me," the phrase we have heard earlier in his sexual torture of Dorothy. This is Jeffrey's and the audience's first indication that the young boy's danger is not just physical, but sexual as well. "Hold him tight for me, boys," Frank tells his henchmen, another suggestion of the erotic implication of this scene. Moaning "Pretty, pretty. Pretty, pretty," Frank spreads crimson lipstick over his face, and then, by kissing Jeffrey, smears lipstick across the boy's face as well. The lipstick recalls the heavily painted faces of both Dorothy and Ben, the two figures with whom Frank has been most intimately connected in the erotic semiology of the film. Frank insists on hearing and chanting along with "Candy-Colored Clown," his name for the Roy Orbison song that Ben sang earlier–another indication of the bisexual SM subtext in Frank's treatment of Jeffrey. Orbison's "In

Dreams," as performed in campy lip-synch by Ben and in poetic chant by Frank, in this context underscores much of the scene's homoerotic logic: "A candy-colored clown they call the Sandman / Tiptoes to my room every night / Just to sprinkle stardust and to whisper / 'Go to sleep, everything is all right.'" For Frank, the song *is* the "candy-colored clown," an image redolent of childhood fantasies, but also highly sexualized, the secret male visitor in the little boy's bedroom at night. The candy image is the trace of the oral-regressive, which homophobic psychoanalytic theory maintained was the origin of homosexual desire in men.[9] The Roy Orbison song is a key to Frank's psyche and his complete immersion in or surrender to a fantasy life: "I close my eyes / Then I drift away / Into the magic night. . . ." Frank's "magic night" is always both "the night world" and a childish dream life.

The revelation of Frank's bisexuality intensifies the audience's perception of Jeffrey's danger, particularly as we begin to see Frank repeating with Jeffrey the nightmarish "foreplay" that he employed in the sex-torture of Dorothy: his breathing in the insect- or cyborg-like gas mask, his pretend-pistol hand motion, and his warning, "Don't you fucking look at me." What is perhaps most frightening about the way that Frank turns suddenly on Jeffrey is that the voyeur with whom the camera has allied us unexpectedly becomes the object of Frank's highly sexualized gaze. In his SM relations with Dorothy, Jeffrey has been exploring a "night world," a "magic night," which he (and we) suddenly discover is not made of his own darkest fantasies, but of Frank's. Frank says both "Baby wants to fuck!" and "It's Daddy, shithead!"; in his dream life, Frank is both baby and daddy. Certainly one disturbing element of Frank's violent patriarchal fantasy is its pervasive infantilism. Frank's oral fixation on the blue velvet material of Dorothy Vallens's dress (and, in particular, the cut-out swatch of it), which he shoves into his own mouth, his victims' mouths, and Dorothy's vagina, is sickly reminiscent of an infant with a favorite blue blanket. This sexual sadist pathology to be "daddy" and "baby" is closely related to Frank's role as the menacing bisexual. The bisexual is the brutal father, the abusive husband, the violent rapist (all familiar figures of male heterosexual power), but he is also the simpering, oral-sadistic mama's boy found in psychoanalytic accounts of homosexuality. These two aspects of virulent biphobia correspond to seemingly less onerous stereotypes about bisexual men in both lesbian and gay and straight cultures: bisexuals as queers with straight privilege, bisexuals as straights with gay chic.

Savage bi male drug criminals like the "AC/DC" junkie of *American Commandos* or Frank Booth are represented as personally violent, and as extremely stylized, but rarely as all that stylish. In this way, they are significantly different from their gay male criminal cohorts in the Hollywood films of the 1980s and '90s, even though the drug-crazed bi male murderer evolved from and continues to relate to the conventions of gay male drug gangsters.[10] Gay drug gangsters typically perpetrate violence through more butch intermediaries and are always flawlessly dressed and coifed, making them less "manly" than their bi male counterparts. Considering bi male drug gangsters in relation to gay men in drug criminal films underscores the ways in which the bisexual male's menace is located in his juxtaposition of dangerous, uncontrolled masculinity and effeminate queerness. As the figure of Frank Booth makes particularly evident, much of the horror represented by the bi male criminal is as a kind of multivalent, polymorphous gender outlaw, a figure whose very presence portends the dissolution of sex and gender systems. In this sense, he threatens to feminize the straight men around him, such as Jeffrey Bellmont. Thus, once again, the bisexual man who kills does not pose a danger of transmitting AIDS, but instead *becomes* AIDS. Like HIV, the bi male killer threatens both contagion and destruction; he is deadly, invasive, self-replicative, transcriptive, and those he marks are set apart from the rest of society.

With the release of *Basic Instinct*, the image of the threatening bisexual junkie that emerged in 1985 to describe male bisexuals had evidently been determined to be applicable to bisexual women as well. Director Paul Verhoeven was well qualified to help articulate this new language around female bisexuality, having already made a film about a deadly woman and a male bisexual, his Dutch-language feature *De Vierde Man/The Fourth Man* (1983). The relationship between misogyny, homophobia, and biphobia in these two works is in many respects similar. In both films, the antagonist is a blonde Salome, a woman whose male lovers have all mysteriously died, and the protagonist is a white man suffering from a mid-life crisis who is divided between his sexual fascination with and his terror of the woman's castrating, witch-like powers. Both films also portray the bisexual character as a sinister, deceitful individual; in the Dutch film, this bisexual is the man (Jeroen Krabbé), whereas in the Hollywood production, the treacherous bisexual and the black widow are one in the same.

The combining in the character of Catherine Tremelle (Sharon Stone) of two distinct narrative conventions–the castrating feminine and the manipulative bisexual–points to the novelty of *Basic Instinct*: the queer woman becomes readable only through the mid-'80s paradigm of the bisexual man as drug-connected criminal. The bisexual woman, too, is in the drug underworld; Catherine's cocaine snorting is an important motif in *Basic Instinct,* and its use marks the ice-pick murder and other scenes in which Catherine's violence or her bisexual erotic life are foregrounded. Moreover, using or abstaining from cocaine appears to be one of the moral centers in the largely amoral universe of the film. Along with her other seductions, the siren unsuccessfully labors to convince the recovering cocaine-addict policeman protagonist to just say yes to a line or two. That Nick (Michael Douglas) never returns to his coke habit as he does to drinking, smoking, police brutality, and heterosexual excesses–the other vices from which he is recovering before he meets Catherine–is an important prerequisite to his retaining the admittedly ambiguous sympathies of the audience. The drug connection is important to *Basic Instinct,* and to the genre as a whole, because during the "Drug Wars" of the 1980s and '90s, illegal drugs functioned as a condensation symbol for a specific mode of criminality which supposedly had to be contained by any means, sacrificing constitutional and social checks on state police power and any moral limit on state or private violence.

The presence of the manipulative bisexual woman sets the lesbian and straight male characters at each other as murderous rivals. Nick asks Catherine's lesbian lover Rocky (Leilani Sarelle) if the two can have a talk "man to man," during which he torments her about what she has just seen–Nick and Catherine having sex–in language powerfully evocative of male heterosexual power: "That was the fuck of my life." Catherine explains to Nick that Rocky always watches her have sex with men, a revelation that chills Nick. But, in fact, *Basic Instinct*'s optics of power are the reverse of what Catherine says. Nick is the voyeur, for whom police surveillance and watching Catherine dress are one in the same. And the real concern raised by the film is not with a lesbian who spies on a straight man and a bi woman, but the straight male gaze extending through the bisexual woman into a lesbian context. There is a "straight porn" aesthetic to the portrayal of women's bisexuality in *Basic Instinct*. In straight-male-oriented video pornography, a standard sex scene is between women who elsewhere in the film have sex with men. Not infrequently, such scenes serve as foreplay to the arrival of a man, who can "join in"–that is, take over–and whose orgasm can, in keeping with the strict discursive conventions of straight video porn, provide a climax and conclusion to the scene. Even absent such an interloper, a man is still the central actor when two women get together in straight pornography because of the implied penetrative gaze of the voyeur, always structured as male. In this way, the "bisexual woman" is constructed as a male heterosexual fantasy, rather than as an autonomous or oppositional erotic agent.

Starting with *Basic Instinct,* "female bisexuality" began to displace "male bisexuality" as the predominant media representation of bisexuals,[11] with bisexual women often offered as commodities for the male gaze. For example, in a February 1996 *Dateline* story, "Walk on the Bi Side," the media-appointed spokesperson who must refute the biphobic claims of both Concerned Women of America's Beverly LaHaye and prominent sexologist Dr. Ruth Westheimer is "Angie," a white 24-year-old whose credentials are that she appears in a *Playboy* spread on bisexual women. This version of female bisexuality is not the representation but the erasure of lesbian/bisexual women's erotic agency–same-sex encounters between women become, through a colonization of gaze and language, extensions of male heterosexuality.

But while Catherine's bisexuality is constructed according to the standards of straight porn, it is also depicted as antisocial, bizarre, violent, and frightening–in other words, as very queer. It is important to see that many of the conventions associated with queer male subjectivity are also linked to the bisexual woman Catherine. In fact, Catherine's effects upon Nick are those of a menacing fag upon the male ingenue. Nick's obsessive pursuit of Catherine pulls him down into a queer, cocaine-using underworld. In one scene, Nick meets Catherine at the bar owned by the man she has killed with an ice pick. The bar is thus immediately linked both to the murder itself and to the BDSM and cocaine demimonde introduced in the ice-pick scene. As the camera moves orgiastically over an array of half-naked, intertwined, dancing bodies–women and women, women and men, men and men–the bar is revealed as a night world of AC/DCs. Catherine and Rocky French kiss passionately and snort coke with a Black gay man. Nick, a cop attempting to be hip, is like Steve, Al Pacino's cop-interloper in the night world of fags in William Friedkin's *Cruising* (1980), and the bi-dyke/cocaine underground into which he has stumbled is similar to the one Steve encounters in leather bars. The sudden transference of historically male homosexual/bisexual codes to women like Catherine is related to important changes in the structure of homophobia and biphobia. Queer nationalism is the lesbian/gay/bi/trans community's progressive response to the post-bi-emergence moment; *Basic Instinct* is the homophobic and biphobic version of the same conceptual shift.

Basic Instinct signaled the appearance of a new tradition in which bi women and lesbians were becoming increasingly susceptible to stereotypical representations that in the earlier period of bi emergence were focused on bisexual men, and that have historically been reserved for gay men. For example, *Chained Heat II* (1993) is set in a prison run by crack-smoking, coke-snorting SM lesbians (Brigitte Nielsen and Jana Svandova), who addict straight women inmates to cocaine in order to seduce them. The image of the sexual predator has long been a common stereotype of gay men, who supposedly draw innocents into drug use in order to indulge their own lusts. In the post-bisexual-emergence moment, in which addiction narrative conventions involving gay white men have been generalized to many other queer subject positions, lesbians have become invested with this Doctor Benway-like[12] power to addict straights, degrade and sexually exploit them, and turn them queer. These blonde SM dykes in lingerie and leather retain *Basic Instinct*'s "straight porn" sensibility, in which the images of women being sexual or erotic together serve heterosexual male fantasies.

The theme of "women behind bars" movies as a genre is the relationship between fantasy and fear in heterosexist imaginings of lesbianism.[13] Unquestionably, *Chained Heat II* belongs to this genre, as is announced by its title, which echoes the most famous women's prison film, Jonathan Demme's 1974 *Caged Heat,* as well as the well-known first *Chained Heat* movie, Paul Nicolas's 1983 version. In the first *Chained Heat,* it is a male warden (John Vernon) who addicts women inmates to cocaine in order to control their sexual labor. "Women's prison" narratives always feature a tough dyke who runs the yard; in the first film, she is a super-Aryan butch lesbian con (Sybil Danning), very much like Brigitte Nielsen's character in the sequel. Traditionally, the jailhouse lesbian, her power controlled by the warden's panoptic authority, becomes another tool in his degradation of the women prisoners. In the post-*Basic Instinct* version, however, the figure of the drug-supplying, pimping warden has been replaced with that of the dyke criminal. A ten-year interval has transformed the terms of lesbians' and bi women's roles in Hollywood and has witnessed a greater investment in the heterosexist representations of queer women–that is to say, an escalation of both fantasies *and* anxieties about lesbians. As is paradigmatic of the post-bisexual-emergence moment, queer women suddenly find themselves endowed in popular culture with powers to do evil to straight women–traditionally a male preserve. But it is important to see that in taking the place of the heterosexual male warden, the lesbian rapist is not actually made in his image, but in that of the gay/bi male drug supplier and sexual exploiter.

In other words, it is important to see in the bisexual crimewave, and especially its internal shift from the bi boy to the bi girl drug-related killer, the rearticulation of the same kinds of identity politics that problematized the relationship of queer liberation movements to feminist praxis in the period of the so-called "great bi debate."[14] In effect, what both the bi crimewave genre and the great bi debate in queer feminism respond to is the same historical process, the sudden volatilization of gay and lesbian communities in the wake of the AIDS epidemic. Throughout the 1970s and early '80s, a tacit feature of the politics of lesbian and gay rights in the U.S. was the development of a separate queer public sphere and the growing certainty that "the gay and lesbian community" and "the heterosexual world" were both geopolitically and demographically discrete, and most theories of social mobilization for queer people, including many progressive lesbian feminist theories, depended on this implied split. It was AIDS which made many heterosexuals conscious of bisexuality and which profoundly problematized the status of gay- or lesbian-identified bisexual people in the lavender districts. Bisexuality emerged in this moment, this sudden political disappearance of the *cordon sanitaire* between straight and lesbian/gay communities. A lesbian feminist politics that sought to disentangle sexual practice and lesbian liberation, as well as a gay male politics that identified public sexual practice with gay liberation, gave way suddenly to a new discourse of sexual *history,* a condition which in turn gave rise to a visible, nameable bisexual identity. Contrary to the conclusions of Marjorie Garber,[15] bisexuality is not intrinsically a narrativity, a "thirdness," or an elision of boundaries that is threatening to culture in general, but rather *appears* to have this significance because of the consequences of this single recent political moment of bi emergence.

In the lavender districts, the main theoretical response in the wake of the moment of bi and transgender emergence was queer nationalism, a far-reaching political project for which the short-lived activism of Queer Nation was in effect only a synecdoche. The New Right's response to these same conditions is the homophobic component of the Drug Wars that have been fought in U.S. popular culture; *Blue Velvet* and *Basic Instinct* are its reactions to the volatilization of the "separate spheres" agreement and the emergence of queer alliance politics, respectively. In the depiction of the night world of AC/DCs, and the need for their surveillance and discipline by vigilantes such as the hero of *American Commandos* and cops such as the protagonist of *Basic Instinct,* there is a clear argument for the recolonization of the lavender districts by heterosexist police power. But in neither the great bi debate in queer communities nor in Hollywood's bi crimewave is bisexuality, or bisexual people, really the issue. What is at stake in both is the organizational plan for the confrontation of heterosexist state power and its discontents.

NOTES

1. Michael du Plessis, "Blatantly Bisexual; or, Unthinking Queer Theory," *RePresenting Bisexualities: Subjects and Cultures of Fluid Desire,* eds. Donald E. Hall and Maria Pramaggiore (New York: New York University Press, 1996), 21.

2. James I. Slaff, *The AIDS Epidemic: How You Can Protect Yourself and Your Family–Why You Must* (New York: Warner Books, 1985), 6, 48-49, 95.

3. Abby Wilkerson, "Homophobia and the Moral Authority of Medicine," *Journal of Homosexuality* 27, nos. 3/4 (1994), 337.

4. Fredric Jameson, *Postmodernism or the Cultural Logic of Late Capitalism* (Durham: Duke University Press, 1991), 294-97.

5. Throughout this essay, "SM" and "sadomasochism" refer to those schemes of representation of SM-related sexual practices in popular Hollywood cinema, which is almost invariably in the domain of psychopathic violence and horror–the world of Geoffrey Dahmer, not Pat Califia. It should be underscored that this representational system does not depict the actual conditions of eros in leather communities and other sites of BDSM practice in queer and straight cultures.

6. This convention raises the interesting question of the relationship between "bisexuals who kill" and the bisexual romantic comedies of the 1990s, in which there are also seemingly bisexual men and women, but again the word "bisexual" is never used, and the characters are forced for plot reasons to "choose" between straight and lesbian/gay identities. Prominent examples of this genre are *Chasing Amy, Three of Hearts, Two Girls and a Guy, Threesome, Wild Things,* and *The Object of My Affection.*

7. Maria Pramaggiore, "Straddling the Screen: Bisexual Spectatorship and Contemporary Narrative Film," *RePresenting Bisexualities,* 272-97.

8. The Leopold-Loeb murder case is a frequently treated movie topic that invariably engages the criminality and pathology of male homosexuality. *Compulsion,* Hitchcock's *Rope* (1948), and Kalin's revisionist *Swoon* (1991) are all examples of this tradition.

9. Charles W. Socarides, *The Overt Homosexual* (New York: Grune and Stratton, 1968), 103-07.

10. This tradition includes, for example, Chucky in *Stick* (1985), Rip in *Less Than Zero* (1987), Sheldon in *Coldfire* (1990), Yves Cloquet in *Naked Lunch* (1991), and the threatening queens from *Cocaine Wars* (1986), *One Man Force* (1989), and *Blood and Concrete* (1990).

11. And after *Basic Instinct*'s release, there were virtually no more male bisexual psychopaths in mainstream Hollywood film. One exception may be found in the ironic presentation of the sociopathic bisexual Xavier Red (Jonathon Schaech) in gay filmmaker Gregg Araki's *The Doom Generation* (1995).

12. Doctor Benway, the archetypal gay male predator, uses drug addiction to convert straight men to homosexuality in William S. Burroughs's *Naked Lunch* (New York: Grove Weidenfeld, 1959, rpt 1992), 26.

13. See, for example, *The Big Doll House* (1971), *The Concrete Jungle* (1982), *Hellhole* (1985), *Red Heat* (1985), *Savage Island* (1985), *Bad Girls' Dormitory* (1986), *The Naked Cage* (1986), and of course the British-made television drama, very popular in the U.S. in the mid- to late 1970s, *Prisoner: Cell Block H.*

14. For bisexual perspectives on the "great bi debate," see Elizabeth Reba Weise, ed., *Closer to Home: Bisexuality and Feminism* (Seattle: Seal Press, 1992) and Loraine Hutchins and Lani Kaahumanu, eds., *Bi Any Other Name: Bisexual People Speak Out* (Boston: Alyson Publications, 1991), 215-357.

15. Marjorie Garber, *Vice Versa: Bisexuality and the Eroticism of Everyday Life* (New York: Simon and Schuster, 1995).

"To Say Yes to Life"

Sexual and Gender Fluidity in James Baldwin's *Giovanni's Room* and *Another Country*

Brett Beemyn

© 2002 by The Haworth Press, Inc. All rights reserved.

[Haworth co-indexing entry note]: "'To Say Yes to Life': Sexual and Gender Fluidity in James Baldwin's *Giovanni's Room* and *Another Country.*" Beemyn, Brett. Co-published simultaneously in *Journal of Bisexuality* (Harrington Park Press, an imprint of The Haworth Press, Inc.) Vol. 2, No. 1, 2002, pp. 55-72; and: *Bisexual Men in Culture and Society* (ed: Brett Beemyn and Erich Steinman) Harrington Park Press, an imprint of The Haworth Press, Inc., 2002, pp. 55-72. Single or multiple copies of this article are available for a fee from The Haworth Document Delivery Service [1-800-342-9678, 9:00 a.m. - 5:00 p.m. (EST). E-mail address: getinfo@haworthpressinc.com].

SUMMARY. James Baldwin's *Giovanni's Room* (1956) and *Another Country* (1962), two of the first works of fiction in the U.S. to openly address same-gender desire, have often been read as "homosexual novels" because the main male characters in each book pursue sexual relationships with other men. Seemingly, it is assumed that any expression of same-gender desire automatically makes a person, and by extension a text, gay. Such a framework is not only short-sighted, but also off-base, as all of the leading male characters in the two works are sexually involved with both men and women. However, simply reinterpreting them as "bisexual novels" would scarcely be more appropriate, for none of the characters explicitly identifies as bisexual, and Baldwin sought to foster meanings that move beyond narrow identity categories, believing that all people had to leave their lives open to both women and men in order to experience life and not be trapped in one aspect of themselves. *[Article copies available for a fee from The Haworth Document Delivery Service: 1-800-342-9678. E-mail address: <getinfo@haworthpressinc. com> Website: <http://www.HaworthPress.com>* © *2002 by The Haworth Press, Inc. All rights reserved.]*

KEYWORDS. Androgyny, *Another Country*, bisexual men, bisexuality, *Giovanni's Room*, James Baldwin

[H]omosexual, bisexual, heterosexual are 20th-century terms which, for me, really have very little meaning. I've never . . . been able to discern exactly where the barriers are. Life being what life is, passion being what passion is. And learning being what that is.

–James Baldwin, from a 1965 interview[1]

[W]e are all androgynous, not only because we are all born of a woman impregnated by the seed of a man but because each of us, helplessly and forever, contains the other–male in female, female in male, white in black and black in white. We are a part of each other.

–James Baldwin, "Here Be Dragons," 1985[2]

James Baldwin's *Giovanni's Room* (1956) and *Another Country* (1962), two of the earliest works of U.S. fiction to focus explicitly on same-gender love, have often been read as "homosexual novels"

because the main male characters in each book pursue sexual relationships with other men. Seemingly, it is assumed that any intragender
desire[3] automatically makes a person, and by extension a text, gay.
Such a framework is not only short-sighted (should *Giovanni's Room*
then be considered his "white novel" because all of the characters are
white?), but also off-base, as all of the leading male characters in the
two works are sexually involved with both men and women. However,
simply reinterpreting them as "bisexual novels" would scarcely be
more appropriate, for none of the characters explicitly identifies as
bisexual and, as the epigraphs above indicate, Baldwin sought to foster meanings that move beyond narrow identity categories. Regardless
of whether someone was bisexual in terms of sexual practice or attraction, he believed that all people had to leave their lives open to both
women and men in order to experience life and not be trapped in one
aspect of themselves.

Baldwin thus placed great value on "bisexual behavior"–sexual
and otherwise–and the breaking down of the gendered boundaries that
can stand in the way of close intragender and intergender relationships. In this sense, his work served as a precursor to the gay liberation
movement's "love whomever you will" philosophy and the initial
bisexual organizing efforts of the early 1970s.[4] But, at the same time,
the two novels perpetuated a number of bisexual stereotypes and reflected the dominant antigay attitudes of the 1950s and early '60s,
including Baldwin's personal ambivalence toward intragender desire.
Consequently, both texts are highly ambiguous and contradictory, re-
ifying biphobic paradigms as much as they challenge them.

How then should *Giovanni's Room* and *Another Country* be interpreted? What do they have to offer a bisexual male reader today who
accepts his sexuality? While keeping in mind that they are clearly
works of their times, I want to offer a reading of these novels that
recognizes the ways in which Baldwin sought to appreciate sexual and
gender fluidity, as manifested through "bisexual" and "androgynous" behaviors, and how these representations are tied to constructions of race. In our era of constant movement, of surfing and shifting
subjectivity, Baldwin reminds us that our position is never fixed, and
that we try to do so at the cost of being fixated on ourselves.

FROM INNOCENCE TO "SOLITARY CONFINEMENT"

Baldwin first focused on intragender desire in "The Preservation of Innocence," a little-known 1949 essay published in a Moroccan journal. Here he not only rejected the notion that homosexuality was unnatural, but also challenged the ability of any sexual or gender identity to be considered natural or unnatural. Such an essentialist belief, he felt, served to ease societal discomfort over sexual and gender differences, which in the case of homosexuality, he linked to anxiety over heterosexual gender relations: the "present debasement and our obsession with [the homosexual] corresponds to the debasement of the relationship between the sexes." Arguing that "[m]en and women have all but disappeared from our popular culture, leaving only this disturbing series of effigies," he particularly criticized the heterosexual relationships in the best-selling novels of James Cain and Raymond Chandler, where "what [the male and female characters] bring to each other is not even passion or sexuality but an unbelievably barren and wrathful grinding."[5]

Five years later, Baldwin turned to an exploration of how the failure to make connections across different genders inhibited same-gender relationships in "Gide as Husband and Homosexual," a review essay of André Gide's *Madeleine* that was subsequently republished as "The Male Prison."[6] Echoing his earlier argument, Baldwin noted that the misogyny of the ultra-macho heroes in the novels of writers like Mickey Spillane prevented them from "get[ting] through to women, which is the only reason their muscles, their fists, and their tommy guns have acquired such fantastic importance" (105). This "prison," though, was not the exclusive domain of heterosexual men whose contempt for women led them to be caught up within themselves. He felt it was also the fate of homosexual men whose fear of women kept them confined to their own gender. In either case, the results, he contended, were the same: "when men can no longer love women they also cease to love or respect or trust each other, which makes their isolation complete" (105). As David Bergman points out, "the target of Baldwin's attack is the rigid exclusivity of either sexual orientation, which he maintains is an 'artificial division' and 'a Western sickness' that limits 'the capacity for experience.'"[7] Gide's troubled marriage, which the French writer admitted stemmed from his failure to accept his attraction to men and to be honest with his wife, exemplified for Baldwin the kind of imprisonment that invariably resulted when the "possibility of entering into communion with another sex" was closed off (105).

The harsh criticism of Gide also reflected Baldwin's own struggle to accept his attraction to both women and men. While, as in "The Preservation of Innocence," he challenged those who argued that homosexuality was unnatural, he admitted at the same time that he was uncomfortable with Gide's openness about his involvement with men:

> And his homosexuality, I felt, was his own affair which he ought to have kept hidden from us, or, if he needed to be so explicit, he ought at least to have managed to be a little more scientific . . . less illogical, less romantic. . . . If he were going to talk about homosexuality at all, he ought, in a word, to have sounded a little less *disturbed.* (102)

As the surprisingly harsh tone of this passage suggests, Baldwin was really the one who was "disturbed," for Gide's experiences raised difficult issues from his own past. At one point in his early twenties, Baldwin had contemplated marriage and even bought a wedding ring. But after reflecting on what he knew then of Gide's unhappy marriage, he decided that he could not risk a similar fate, that his greater attraction to men meant that it was "many light-years too late" for such a relationship. The ring ended up in the Hudson River.[8]

The value that Baldwin placed on being able to relate to both women and men, as well as his personal ambivalence toward homosexuality, were also readily apparent in *Giovanni's Room,* his second novel, which was published two years after "The Male Prison" but begun a decade earlier.[9] Initially, Baldwin had sought to begin a serious exploration of intragender desire in his first novel, *Go Tell It on the Mountain* (1953), including an ending in which the teenage male protagonist acknowledged his homosexuality and "[said], in effect, 'I want a man.'"[10] But "no publisher would touch it. They flatly rejected it or suggested massive cuts, primarily of the homosexual content." The novel was finally published by Alfred A. Knopf, but not before Baldwin submerged the homoerotic element and dropped the concluding scene.[11]

With *Giovanni's Room,* Baldwin substantially upped the stakes, for "there was no way the theme of homosexuality could be cut out of this second novel. It was a bisexual love story and he realized as he wrote it that this time he was holding back nothing but was being 'straight from the shoulder' about his life and concerns."[12] If the homosexuality in *Go Tell It on the Mountain* had been an anathema to publishers, the bisexual focus of *Giovanni's Room* was perhaps less acceptable in the 1950s, given that even the developing homophile movement was ambivalent at best toward bisexuality. While bisexual men were not explicitly excluded from the Mattachine Society, as they had been from Chicago's Society for Human Rights, the first U.S. homophile group, which existed briefly in the 1920s,[13] they were still frequently marginalized and their right to be included was, at times, hotly debated. For example, during more than a decade of publishing, the group's newsletter, *The Mattachine Review,* ran just one article about bisexuality, and only two others even acknowledged the existence of people who were attracted to both women and men.[14]

The fact that bisexual men faced rejection from both the dominant society and the emerging homosexual movement may not have deterred Baldwin, but the lack of any identifiable supportive audience did concern his agent, who advised him that a book like *Giovanni's Room* would ruin his career and that he was better off burning the manuscript. Nevertheless, she sent the work off to Knopf, which rejected it as "repugnant" and suggested instead "another 'Negro' novel" along the lines of *Go Tell It on the Mountain.* Several other publishers likewise turned down the book because of its content before it finally was accepted by a smaller, less well-known press.[15]

The wish that he produce "another 'Negro' novel" points to how *Giovanni's Room* has typically been treated as an aberration among Baldwin's fiction and has received less critical attention in studies of African American literature, because it includes no Black characters, as well as few exclusively heterosexual ones.[16] Yet, as Robert F. Reid-Pharr persuasively argues, "the question of blackness, precisely because of its very apparent absence, screams out at the turn of every page."[17] Moreover, by focusing on the shift from Black characters, critics ignore the ways in which the novel develops many of the ideas that Baldwin first raised in his essays, most notably in "The Preservation of Innocence" and "The Male Prison." Far from being an anomaly, *Giovanni's Room* was in keeping with Baldwin's previous work, expressing themes that he could only obliquely address in *Go Tell It on the Mountain,* and which he would subsequently return to in his third novel, *Another Country.*

Although *Giovanni's Room* contains no African American characters, it by no means ignores race. In the novel's opening paragraph, Baldwin situates his protagonist, David, in history as a white American: "I watch my reflection in the darkening gleam of the window pane. . . . My ancestors conquered a continent, pushing across death-laden plains, until they came to an ocean which faced away from Europe into a darker past."[18] David's own struggle is to confront that "darker past" and not be confined by his whiteness, specifically the white American myth of innocence, which Baldwin considered one of the greatest impediments to whites being able to understand themselves.[19] But David is unwilling to face himself in the glass's opaqueness–"to crack that mirror and be free" (247)–so he can neither accept his attraction to men nor find satisfaction in relationships with women. Having internalized the homophobic attitudes of the dominant society, the pattern for his isolation is set from his first sexual experience–a relationship with Joey, a "dark," "very nice boy," who was his best friend (8). Initially, David feels that "a lifetime would not be long enough" for them to love each other (11); however, he flees the next morning from both Joey and his own feelings, seeing in his desire for the body of another boy an uncleanliness that would forever deny him access to white male privilege: "That body suddenly seemed the black opening of a cavern in which I would be tortured till madness came, in which I would lose my manhood. A cavern opened in my mind, black, . . . full of dirty words. . . . I thought I saw my future in that cavern" (12).

David's experience with Joey foreshadows his relationship with Giovanni, whom he meets in Paris while trying to reassure himself that he *really* was innocent, untainted, and not attracted to men by immersing himself in the gay underworld that he most loathed and feared:[20]

> while this milieu was certainly anxious enough to claim me, I was intent on proving, to them and to myself, that I was not of their company. I did this by being in their company a great deal and manifesting toward all of them a tolerance which placed me, I believed, above suspicion. (33)

Although David has a fiancée, Hella, he remains unsettled and unsure of his desires, emphasized by the fact that he becomes homeless on the day he meets Giovanni. Immediately moving into Giovanni's room, David looks to find a haven and an outlet for his suppressed intragender feelings. But he can no more find a home there than he can with Hella because, like the disheveled character of the room itself, he is unable to resolve his mixed emotions or overcome his belief in the dirtiness of same-gender love. Similar to the homophobia evoked by his feelings for Joey, he fears that Giovanni will awaken in him "a beast [that] would never go to sleep again" and lead him into "following all kinds of boys down God knows what dark avenues, into what dark places" (122). As this passage demonstrates, Baldwin's use of darkness, like his treatment of sexuality, is dialectic: it represents both the danger of David being condemned to a life of isolation in a loveless gay world and, if he could allow himself to risk loving the dark-skinned Giovanni (or Joey before him), the possibility of salvation through overcoming his racial ignorance and sexual denial.

The opportunity that Giovanni provides for David to move beyond himself and to accept his sexual attraction to both women and men is recognized by Jacques, who serves as "the spokesperson for the homosexual underworld" and as the most direct voice of Baldwin in the novel.[21] Even before David goes home with Giovanni, Jacques tells him that he must overcome his self-denial or face seeing his worst fears come true:

> love him and let him love you. Do you think anything else under heaven really matters? . . . And if you think of [intragender relationships] as dirty, then they *will* be dirty–they will be dirty

because you will be giving nothing, you will be despising your
flesh and his. But you can make your time together anything but
dirty, you can give each other something which will make both of
you better–forever–if you will *not* be ashamed, if you will only
not play it safe. . . . You play it safe long enough . . . and you'll
end up trapped in your own dirty body, forever and forever and
forever–like me. (83-84)

The message, though, is lost on David, whose inability to love anything except his purity, "his mirror," destroys not only himself but
also Giovanni and Hella. While David ultimately recognizes that he
loves Giovanni and has been lying to himself, the admission comes
too late for Giovanni, who is about to be executed for a murder that
has as much to do with David's abandonment as it does with Giovanni's desperation. David's willingness, finally, to accept the love of
another man may also be too late for David himself, for Giovanni's
impending death parallels his own emotional death. At the end of the
novel, as he prepares to leave the house in which he has imprisoned
himself while awaiting Giovanni's execution, David admits that his
body too "is under sentence of death. . . . It is trapped in [his] mirror as
it is trapped in time and it hurries toward revelation" (247).

David's self-revelation about his love for Giovanni does offer some
hope that he can divest himself of false innocence and break out of his
isolation, and the novel's final scene seems to leave this possibility
open. Ending his self-imposed exile, he sees a group of women and
men awaiting the morning bus, who are "very vivid beneath the awak-
ening sky" (248). The vividness here suggests that David is really
looking at others for the first time, and the fact that the scene includes
both women and men is telling. As Reed Woodhouse notes, "Baldwin
has been careful to put both men and women in his final tableau, as if
to say, 'This combination of male and female is precisely what makes
for a real, not illusory, world.'"[22]

However, before David can join this world and perhaps end his
self-entrapment, he has to resolve his relationship with Giovanni. He
tears up the note from Jacques that informed him of the date of Giovanni's execution, throwing the pieces to the wind. But demonstrating
that he can no longer ignore the "darker past" or deny his intragender

desire in the future, the scraps are not so easily disposed of: "as I turn and begin walking toward the waiting people, the wind blows some of them back on me" (248). That the note is from Jacques, the personification of all that David holds contemptible about the gay social world, also reinforces the need for David to accept his attraction to both women and men and to listen to Jacques's (indeed, Baldwin's) advice that to love others, to move beyond oneself, necessarily involves taking risks.[23]

FROM SELF TO OTHER COUNTRIES

While it is uncertain whether David will succeed in freeing himself from himself, Baldwin is much less ambiguous in *Another Country,* which even more thoroughly explores the cost of failing to love and the importance of maintaining meaningful connections within and across categories of race, gender, and sexuality. Whereas *Giovanni's Room* is told through David's voice, *Another Country* has what Robert Corber describes as "multiple centers of intelligence." He argues that by frequently shifting between the viewpoints of characters of different races, classes, genders, and sexualities, the novel encourages readers to move outside of themselves and to identify and develop political solidarity across several axes of difference.[24] The result is the breaking down of rigid identity categories and the recognition of individual complexity, which Baldwin considered necessities of human existence that had to be represented in literature:

> In overlooking, denying, evading [our] complexity, . . . we are diminished and we perish; only within this web of ambiguity, paradox, this hunger, danger, darkness, can we find at once ourselves and the power that will free us from ourselves. It is this power of revelation which is the business of the novelist, this journey toward a more vast reality which must take precedence over all other claims.[25]

Ironically, while readers are urged to see the need to move beyond their own narrow subjectivities, the characters in *Another Country* are rarely able to identify with each other or to grasp the complexities of race, gender, and sexuality. This is especially the case for the main male characters: Rufus, Vivaldo, and Eric. All three are involved in sexual relationships with both women and men, often across racial lines, yet are incapable at times of relating to anyone, including themselves. In a country dominated by rigid categories, they are unable to embrace difference–to know "other countries."[26]

Of the three, Rufus is the most trapped by racial and sexual stereotypes. Because he cannot overcome the images that society has of him as a Black man who is involved in relationships with white women and men, he can respect neither himself nor others, and ends up taking his own life early in the novel. Like David in *Giovanni's Room,* Rufus is both intrigued and repulsed by Eric's desire for him; he "treat[s] him as nothing more than a hideous sexual deformity," yet it is Eric, along with Leona, his most recent lover, and Ida, his sister, whom he thinks of with fondness and regret before he commits suicide.[27] Similarly, Rufus's relationship with Leona is filled with ambivalence because neither can see the other beyond their race and gender identities. She "had not been a deformity [but] he had used against her the very epithets he had used against Eric, and in the very same way" (46). When Eric recognizes that Rufus had consented to a sexual relationship in part to be able to despise himself and Eric more completely, he flees literally to another country. Leona eventually reaches a similar conclusion about her relationship with Rufus, but, as a working-class white woman, she has less social mobility than Eric; her flight leads her to insanity.

Although Rufus dies early in *Another Country,* "his presence remains throughout the novel, reminding and offering hints to the other characters about the cost of socially constructed identity categories."[28] Yet, if Rufus is the book's spiritual center, Eric is its physical center, not simply because he has sex with most of the other characters, but because he ultimately does what Rufus (and David before him) is unable to do; he breaks through the racial, gender, and sexual dichotomies that prevent him from clearly seeing himself and reaching out to others. His refusal to be limited by categories is recognized by Vivaldo, for example, when he first sees Eric acting in a film:

[F]or the first time, [he] caught a glimpse of who Eric really was. . . . It was the face of a man, of a tormented man. Yet, in precisely the way that great music depends, ultimately, on great silence, this masculinity was defined, and made powerful, by something which was not masculine. But it was not feminine, either, and something in Vivaldo resisted the word *androgynous*. . . . [I]t was a face which suggested, resonantly, in the depths, the truth about our natures. (330)

The fact that he is acting, but still being more true to human nature than the other characters, demonstrates the extent to which Eric has moved beyond binary meanings–even "androgynous" is seen as a limiting label–and just how trapped the others are by such meanings.

Eric too was initially ensconced in narrow sexual and gender categories. In the beginning of the novel, he resides in the South of France, having created his own Garden of Eden with his appropriately-named lover Yves by excluding the heterosexual world outside. But recognizing that it is "a rented garden," Eric must choose between remaining in his homosocial paradise, eternally cut off from the rest of humanity, or reentering the larger world to pursue the acting break that he has been hoping for, a leading role in a Broadway production of the *Happy Hunting Ground* (183). New York, though, has been anything but a happy hunting ground for Eric. Besides being the site of his failed relationship with Rufus, it was also where, instead of mutual love and sexual pleasure, he had found an "army of lonely men who had used him . . . [as] the receptacle of an anguish which he could scarcely believe was in the world" (211).

While David goes to France because he "wanted to find [him]self" (31) and to hide from his sexual desires, Eric decides to return to this country to avoid losing himself and to face his fears about losing Yves and again encountering male partners who are incapable of affection. But continuing to operate from an essentialist framework, he soon becomes involved with Cass, hoping that this affair will be his "opportunity to change" and will enable him to avoid the "chaos" of same-gender relationships (339). However, as much as he would like to fall in love with a woman and "become heterosexual," he realizes through his passionate one-night relationship with Vivaldo that he is simply using Cass to avoid facing himself and the complexities of sexual identity. Intimacy with Vivaldo enables Eric to understand that he can obtain love from other men, and the novel concludes with Eric rejecting the dichotomy of sexual choice.

For Vivaldo, his relationship with Eric also serves a critical function, as he had previously told another man who was interested in sex that his attraction to men was "a long time ago" (315). Moreover, until this point, he "was made too uneasy by what he knew of Eric's relation to Rufus" to be able to discuss it with either one, even though he continually professes to have loved Rufus after his death (191). But it is precisely because Vivaldo is forced by Ida to recognize that he did not really know her brother and had done nothing to prevent his death that he becomes sexually involved with Eric. Because Eric had made love with Rufus and taken the risks that Vivaldo had been too afraid to take in order to become close to him, Vivaldo's relationship with Eric serves as a means for Vivaldo to relinquish his own emotional safety and to love Rufus by proxy.[29]

Prior to engaging in sex, Vivaldo reveals to Eric that he might have "saved" Rufus if he had held him and shown love for him when Rufus most needed to be comforted–"if I'd just reached out that quarter of an inch between us on that bed" (342-43). This "quarter inch" is symbolic of the racial and sexual divide between them, for like David, Vivaldo seeks to maintain his sense of purity, preventing him from being able to identify across lines of difference and to connect with others. He thus continues to see homosexuality as a threat to his manhood and to feel that he is "far beyond the reach of anything so banal and corny as color" (133). Ultimately, he overcomes his literal and figurative separation through reaching across the bed to Eric. Yet, demonstrating that Vivaldo is still not ready to abandon his false innocence, their embrace begins subconsciously, as part of a dream in which Vivaldo holds and expresses his love for Rufus, as Rufus is trying to kill him. The dream recalls the earlier scene on the bed, which had occurred after Rufus had threatened Vivaldo, and serves as a visceral manifestation of his guilt: Rufus seeks vengeance for Vivaldo's failure to see him for who he is.

The subsequent sexual relationship between Vivaldo and Eric also has a dream-like quality. In a sense, it is a "dream come true" for Vivaldo, who believes that "he had created his dream in order to create this opportunity; he had brought about something that he had long desired," despite his previously expressed desires to the contrary (383). Still, Vivaldo is ambivalent about the relationship, seeing it "as strangely and insistently double-edged, it was like making love in the midst of mirrors, or it was like death by drowning. But it was also like music, the highest, sweetest, loneliest reeds" (385). The reference to "mirrors" invokes David's struggle to crack the "mirror" of his pure self-image that prevents him from seeing himself and others more clearly, and, like David, Vivaldo can only be free if he overcomes his association of same-gender love "with the humiliation and the debasement of one male by another" (384).

In line with Baldwin's dictum that people open their lives emotionally to both women and men, it does not matter that Vivaldo and Eric's relationship "may never happen again" (387). The fact that Vivaldo has been able to love and be loved by another man means that he can now "say Yes to life"–to use Baldwin's description in *Giovanni's Room* (6)–and can transcend narrow identity categories. Vivaldo himself recognizes the significance of this change, thinking after having sex with Eric that "no matter what happened to him from now until he died, . . . there was a man in the world who loved him. All of his hope, which had grown so pale, flushed into life again" (387).

By risking to know Eric, Vivaldo is finally able to know some of what Rufus went through and can honestly say for the first time that he loves him. At this point, he is also able to know and love Ida, who has accurately challenged Vivaldo throughout the novel about "how you can talk about love when you don't want to know what's happening. . . . How can you love somebody you don't know anything about?" (324-25). She forces Vivaldo to recognize that Rufus would still be alive if he had not been born Black, thereby "stroking his innocence out of him" (431). As if to signal that Vivaldo has now freed himself from his own narrow subjectivity, a long-sought element for his novel occurs to him that "illuminated, justified, clarified everything" (427).

Eric's life is also clarified when he is able to face himself and make meaningful connections with both women and men. On the morning following his night with Vivaldo, he receives word first that he is soon to star in a movie and then that Yves will be arriving the next day. In sharp contrast to his feelings when he first came to New York, when Eric welcomes Yves to this country, "[h]e looked very much at ease, at home" (435). Like Vivaldo, he realizes that even if his relationship with Yves should end, he would still be able to love and be loved.

"[L]ove between any two human beings would not be possible," Baldwin argued, "did we not have available to us the spiritual resources of both sexes," by which he meant being able to relate to both men and women, including the male and female within ourselves-what he labeled androgyny, "[the] man in every woman and [the] woman in every man."[30] While this ability to connect with people of different genders–along with people of different races–may be expressed sexually, "bisexual behavior," as conceived by Baldwin, transcends the physical. Thus Eric may never again be sexually involved with a woman, but can still love women and recognize that part of himself. At the other extreme, David and Rufus have sexual relationships with both women and men, yet fail tragically in their attempts to make meaningful connections with anyone else, due to David's inability to accept and move beyond himself and Rufus's inability to know himself outside of the stereotypes that society imposes on him. The challenge that Baldwin calls us to is to see ourselves and each other beyond simplistic categories and narrow, isolated identities, for only through such a vision is love truly possible.

NOTES

1. James Mossman, "Race, Hate, Sex, and Colour: A Conversation with James Baldwin and Colin MacInnes," *Conversations with James Baldwin,* eds. Fred L. Standley and Louis H. Pratt (Jackson: University Press of Mississippi, 1989), 54-55 [originally published in *Encounter* 25 (July 1965): 55-60].

2. James Baldwin, "Here Be Dragons," *The Price of the Ticket: Collected Non-fiction, 1948-1985* (New York: St. Martin's, 1985), 690 [originally published as "Freaks and the American Ideal of Manhood," *Playboy* (January 1985)].

3. Recognizing that referring to one aspect of gender as "sex" has the effect of reinforcing a kind of biological determinism that ignores other components of gender and erases gender fluidity, I use the terms "intragender" and "intergender" throughout this essay, rather than "same sex" and "opposite/other sex," to describe desires and behaviors. Perhaps it is for similar reasons that another Baldwin scholar uses the

same language: Marlon B. Ross, "White Fantasies of Desire: Baldwin and the Racial Identities of Sexuality," *James Baldwin Now,* ed. Dwight A. McBride (New York: New York University Press, 1999), 13-55. For a thoughtful discussion of the assumptions underlying the use of "sex" to stand-in for "gender," see Kate Bornstein, *My Gender Workbook* (New York: Routledge, 1998).

4. For an examination of the philosophies of the gay and bisexual movements in the early 1970s, see Amanda Udis-Kessler, "Identity/Politics: A History of the Bisexual Movement," and Stephen Donaldson, "The Bisexual Movement's Beginnings in the 70s: A Personal Retrospective," *Bisexual Politics: Theories, Queries, and Visions,* ed. Naomi Tucker (Binghamton, NY: Harrington Park Press, 1995), 17-30 and 31-45.

5. James Baldwin, "The Preservation of Innocence," *OUT/LOOK* 2 (Fall 1989): 41, 43 [originally published in *Zero* 1 (Summer 1949): 14-22].

6. James Baldwin, "The Male Prison," *The Price of the Ticket,* 101-05 [originally published as "Gide as Husband and Homosexual," *New Leader* 37 (December 13, 1954): 18-20]. All citations to the essay will refer to *The Price of the Ticket* edition.

7. David Bergman, "The African and the Pagan in Gay Black Literature," *Sexual Sameness: Textual Differences in Lesbian and Gay Writing,* ed. Joseph Bristow (New York: Routledge, 1992), 154.

8. Baldwin, "Here Be Dragons," 685; W.J. Weatherby, *James Baldwin: Artist on Fire* (New York: Dell, 1989), 69. Baldwin would later incorporate aspects of this experience into *Another Country*: Eric buys cufflinks for Rufus with the money he was supposed to use for wedding rings.

9. David Leeming, *James Baldwin: A Biography* (New York: Alfred A. Knopf, 1994), 52.

10. Weatherby, *James Baldwin,* 109.

11. Gregory Woods, *A History of Gay Literature: The Male Tradition* (New Haven, CT: Yale University Press, 1998), 293; Weatherby, *James Baldwin,* 133. For an examination of the remaining homosexual element of *Go Tell It on the Mountain,* see Emmanuel S. Nelson, "The Novels of James Baldwin: Struggles of Self-Acceptance," *Journal of American Culture* 8 (Winter 1985): 12.

12. Weatherby, *James Baldwin,* 133.

13. John Loughery, *The Other Side of Silence: Men's Lives and Gay Identities: A Twentieth-Century History* (New York: Henry Holt, 1998), 54. Ironically, the vice-president of the Society for Human Rights was a married bisexual man who kept this fact hidden from other members. His need for secrecy contributed to the Society's demise: his wife divulged the group's existence to a social worker, who in turn notified the Chicago police department, who arrested its leaders.

14. Bisexuality, though, was discussed within Mattachine itself, and could lead to contentious debates. For example, when the findings of Kinsey's research–showing that many people have sexual experiences with both women and men over the course of their lives–were raised in a 1968 meeting, Frank Kameny, the leader of Mattachine Society-Washington, responded that "people are always either one or the other" and that "those who engage in sexual acts with men and women both are simply 'closet queens' who use their heterosexual acts as a facade to hide their homosexual behavior." In response, the president of Mattachine Society-New York, Dick Leitsch, ar-

gued that bisexuals were a primary constituency for the group, citing not only scientific research, but also the men who sought help from Mattachine and his own sexual history. Toby Marotta, *The Politics of Homosexuality* (Boston: Houghton Mifflin, 1981), 60-61.

15. James Campbell, *Talking at the Gates: A Life of James Baldwin* (New York: Viking, 1991), 104-05; Weatherby, *James Baldwin,* 135, 138.

16. Although *Giovanni's Room* is generally overlooked or dismissed in African American literary and cultural studies, the novel, as Marlon B. Ross points out, "has gained a central place in (white) gay culture and is often a focus of attention in (white) gay studies." Ross, "White Fantasies of Desire," 16. For example, Reed Woodhouse begins *Unlimited Embrace: A Canon of Gay Fiction, 1945-1995* (Amherst: University of Massachusetts Press, 1998) with a discussion of *Giovanni's Room,* "the first gay book [he] ever read," rather than earlier works like John Horne Burns's *The Gallery* and Gore Vidal's *The City and the Pillar.*

17. Robert F. Reid-Pharr, "Tearing the Goat's Flesh: Crisis, Homosexuality, Abjection, and the Production of a Late-Twentieth-Century Black Masculinity," *Novel Gazing: Queer Readings in Fiction,* ed. Eve Kosofsky Sedgwick (Durham, NC: Duke University Press, 1997), 369.

18. James Baldwin, *Giovanni's Room* (1956; New York: Dial Press, 1962), 3. All citations will be taken from this edition.

19. See James Baldwin, "The Fire Next Time," *The Price of the Ticket,* 334, and "The Black Boy Looks at the White Boy," *The Price of the Ticket,* 290.

20. Reid-Pharr, "Tearing the Goat's Flesh," 371.

21. Yasmin Y. DeGout, "Dividing the Mind: Contradictory Portraits of Homoerotic Love in *Giovanni's Room,*" *African American Review* 26 (1992): 431.

22. Woodhouse, *Unlimited Embrace,* 33.

23. Ibid., 34.

24. Robert J. Corber, *Homosexuality in Cold War America: Resistance and the Crisis of Masculinity* (Durham, NC: Duke University Press, 1997), 178.

25. James Baldwin, "Everybody's Protest Novel," *The Price of the Ticket,* 29.

26. For a fuller discussion of the cost to the characters of adhering to rigid categories, see James A. Dievler, "Sexual Exiles: James Baldwin and *Another Country,*" *James Baldwin Now,* 161-83.

27. James Baldwin, *Another Country* (1962; New York: Vintage, 1993), 46. All citations will be taken from this edition.

28. Dievler, "Sexual Exiles," 171.

29. Leeming, *James Baldwin,* 203.

30. Baldwin, "Here Be Dragons," 677.

Invisible Lives

Addressing Black Male Bisexuality in the Novels of E. Lynn Harris

Lisa Frieden

© 2002 by The Haworth Press, Inc. All rights reserved.

[Haworth co-indexing entry note]: "Invisible Lives: Addressing Black Male Bisexuality in the Novels of E. Lynn Harris." Frieden, Lisa. Co-published simultaneously in *Journal of Bisexuality* (Harrington Park Press, an imprint of The Haworth Press, Inc.) Vol. 2, No. 1, 2002, pp. 73-90; and: *Bisexual Men in Culture and Society* (ed: Brett Beemyn and Erich Steinman) Harrington Park Press, an imprint of The Haworth Press, Inc., 2002, pp. 73-90. Single or multiple copies of this article are available for a fee from The Haworth Document Delivery Service [1-800-342-9678, 9:00 a.m. - 5:00 p.m. (EST). E-mail address: getinfo@ haworthpressinc.com].

SUMMARY. *Invisible Life* is an important U.S. novel for being one of the first to forefront black male bisexuality and the often complex connections between sexual behavior and sexual identity for men of color. In order to understand how *Invisible Life* frames sexual identity, this article first examines some of the important issues involving male bisexuality within black communities and how the politics and economics of the publishing industry have influenced the publication of novels by and about gay and bisexual black men. The article then provides an analysis of the novel itself and its portrayals of black male bisexuality. Finally, the article discusses how Harris's later novels have rejected bisexuality in favor of affirming black gay identities. *[Article copies available for a fee from The Haworth Document Delivery Service: 1-800-342-9678. E-mail address: <getinfo@haworthpressinc.com> Website: <http://www.HaworthPress. com> © 2002 by The Haworth Press, Inc. All rights reserved.]*

KEYWORDS. African Americans, bisexual men, bisexuality, black literature, E. Lynn Harris, *Invisible Life*

But was I gay or bisexual and what was the difference? Many gay men viewed bisexuality with misgivings. The feeling was that bisexuality was a cop-out. That you were one or the other, no in-between. Did I hang on to my bisexuality because it was more acceptable?[1]

Few novels published in the United States have described the experiences of behaviorally bisexual men of color. In fact, not until 1991, with the publication of E. Lynn Harris's *Invisible Life,* did a novel have black male bisexuality as its central theme.[2] Though not a work of "great" fiction, *Invisible Life* is important for forefronting a discussion that has been occurring less openly in black communities for years. *Invisible Life* addresses how the terms "gay" and "bisexual" are defined, highlighting the often-complex connections between sexual behavior and sexual identity for men involved in same- and other-sex relationships. Most of the novel focuses on its narrator, Raymond, who struggles to decide, "was I gay or bisexual and what was the difference?" In the end, he finds that "gay" and "bisexual" tend to imply stable identities that cannot adequately describe his sexuality or the sexuality of other black men.

Researchers have likewise recognized the inadequacy of the language of sexuality. As Martin Manalansan notes, "[e]ven the phrase, men who have sex with men, is unable to capture the complex ways in which different cultures provide meanings and structures for such phenomena."[3] In the absence of more accurate terminology, I will use "gay" and "bisexual" in this essay, but I will be careful to differentiate between sexual identity and sexual behavior. Sexual identity implies a level of stability and uniformity that sexual behavior does not, as sexual practices can vary with each individual instance. In order to understand how *Invisible Life* frames sexual identity, I first examine some of the important issues involving male bisexuality within black communities and how the politics and economics of the publishing industry have influenced the publication of novels by and about gay and bisexual black men. I then turn my attention to an analysis of the novel itself and its portrayals of black male bisexuality. Finally, I discuss how Harris's later novels have rejected bisexuality in favor of affirming black gay identities.

NOT GAY, NOT STRAIGHT:
RACE, CLASS, CULTURE, AND INVISIBLE IDENTITIES

An integral part of the gay rights movement of the 1970s involved interrogating and revising the normative cultural definitions of sexual identity. "Homosexuality," which had been coined in the nineteenth century to describe a supposedly pathological sexual disorder, was dismissed in favor of the term "gay."[4] This new terminology not only reflected a newly empowered sense of individual male homosexual identity, but also served to encapsulate the growing communities of men who shared this sense of sexual identity. Self-demarcated neighborhoods in New York City and San Francisco, for example, openly and proudly identified themselves as "gay communities." However, as the gay rights movement solidified in the mid- and late 1970s, "gay" largely came to signify a white, middle-class identity, thus silencing the experiences and narratives of the majority of men who have sex with other men.

Clearly, cultural contexts influence people's sexual identities.[5] In the United States, race and socioeconomic status have had an especial-

ly significant impact on how sexual identities are developed and artic-
ulated, and these forces are perhaps most visibly manifested in black
communities, where at times they have conflicting effects. On the one
hand, as Benjamin Bowser writes, "[t]he capitalist nature of American
society has reduced Black male and female relations into commodities
where men and women treat themselves as sexual objects."[6] On the
other hand, white racist stereotypes about black sexuality have led
some African Americans, particularly some members of the middle
class, to de-emphasize their sexual identities. Phillip Brian Harper
remarks that "[i]ndeed, some middle-class blacks have colluded in
this defusing of black sexuality, attempting to explode whites' stereotypes of blacks as oversexed by stifling discussion of black sexuality
generally."[7]

Exacerbated by homophobia and biphobia, the silence surrounding
black male bisexuality has been particularly strong, with the conse-
quence that some black bisexual men feel they must lead double lives
in order to fit into seemingly heterosexual black communities. Laura
Randolph argues that "mainstream Black America must shoulder at
least partial responsibility for the code of secrecy many Black bisexual
men say they are compelled to live by."[8] Compounding the invisibility
of black male bisexuals is the lack of research on their lives. Indeed,
"[b]ecause the sexual behavior of minority men who engage in bisexual activities has rarely been studied," Lynda Doll et al. found that
estimations of "the extent of bisexual behavior among black Americans is largely derived from surveillance reports of nonwhite AIDS
cases."[9] Thus what little data exists on black male bisexuality reinforces the stereotype that most bisexual men have or will develop
AIDS, as well as the accompanying myth that they likely became
infected through covert sexual relationships with other men.

The invisibility of black bisexual men is also readily apparent in
bisexual social and political organizing. Bisexuals in the U.S. are
generally still in the early stages of community development, but the
cultural institutions that have been created thus far (national and regional organizations, publications, Internet sites, etc.) are predominantly white. As a result, some black bisexual men feel torn in their
allegiances. When both black gay and predominantly white bisexual

communities speak only partially to their experiences and needs, how can they bring together their racial and sexual identities? Ironically, many gay black men have experienced a similar split in their lives, leading them to begin to form their own communities.[10] "Because the gay community in the United States is viewed by some blacks as being dominated by white men," write Doll et al., "in some communities there may also be an inherent tension between the development of ties to both the black and gay communities, respectively."[11] Additionally, as Charles Stewart has remarked, gay culture is typically separated by race: "in most American cities the gay community is largely white and segregated, with most black gays participating in its institutions only occasionally if at all. This is particularly true of working-class blacks and those who live in predominantly black neighborhoods."[12]

THE LITERARY MARKETPLACE

With the tremendous growth and development of white gay communities since the 1970s, presses that cater to lesbian and gay readerships have also proliferated. Indeed, as Victoria Brownworth has noted, "[g]ay and lesbian literature is the publishing trend of the '90's."[13] Until fairly recently, sympathetic editors at large mainstream publishing houses, like St. Martin's Michael Denneny, had to take it upon themselves to promote particular lesbian and gay books; otherwise, these works would have faced almost certain rejection. But as smaller lesbian and/or gay presses, such as Naiad, Firebrand, and Alyson, demonstrated its marketability, major houses became much more willing to publish literature by openly lesbian, gay, and bisexual authors, and the number of such books has skyrocketed.

Despite this dramatic increase, the range of works available remains extremely limited. "The booming trade in gay books," writes Brownworth, "is still the domain of a select few gay white men."[14] According to Michele Karlsberg, a book publicist who worked with such well-known black gay authors as Assoto Saint and Melvin Dixon, among publishers, "[t]here is an underlying racist and classist idea that blacks don't read and buy books."[15]

Such assumptions by the gay publishing industry have led to significant silences, particularly with respect to the experiences of gay and bisexual men of color. "Read any good black gay fiction lately?" asks black gay novelist Steve Corbin. He argues that "[u]nless one is literature-savvy, one could easily subscribe to the misconception that African-American gay male fiction–and its writers–had died along with James Baldwin in 1987."[16] Although several black female novelists have become household names in recent years, black male novelists, and especially black gay novelists, according to Corbin, have had difficulty finding places to publish their work. Corbin extensively criticizes what he perceived to be the racist assumptions and practices of both straight and gay presses in the early 1990s, many of which remain unchanged today:

> We can presuppose myriad perennial assumptions and baseless theories to justify these classic patterns. Black gay literature isn't commercially viable; black literature is second-rate; black literature has no audience; only blacks are interested in black art; blacks don't read; and, finally, that one black voice is representative and encompassing of all black people, which succinctly explains why we have been doomed to celebrate one solitary literary icon at a time, posturing as the "flavor of the month."[17]

Although Corbin dismisses as racist the assumption by white editors that black authors lack the time and financial resources to write extended works of fiction, time and money *are* issues for some writers of color. Nancy Bereano, the publisher of Firebrand Books, a small lesbian press which publishes many lesbians of color, insists that "[w]hen we're talking about the big [publishing] houses, they want novels, and many writers of color don't have the time or money to write novels."[18] Corbin does accurately point out, though, that because most editors are white men, they do not identify with the experiences of black gays and/or may find these experiences threatening to their own notions of identity–racial, sexual, or otherwise.[19] Barbara Smith, the publisher of Kitchen Table: Women of Color Press, agrees, arguing that texts by lesbians and gays of color include "an inherent critique in what we write of the society, and many editors take that critique personally."[20] Thus the lack of black editors who might positively respond to and promote the publication of novels by black gay and bisexual men has also contributed to their invisibility.

Black gay men, though, have achieved relatively greater visibility through literary and artistic forms outside of the novel. For example, Joseph Beam's *In the Life: A Black Gay Anthology,* Essex Hemphill's *Brother to Brother: New Writings by Black Gay Men,* the collections published by the group Other Countries, and genre-specific anthologies such as Assoto Saint's *The Road Before Us: 100 Gay Black Poets* and Bruce Morrow and Charles H. Rowell's *Shade: An Anthology of Fiction by Gay Men of African Descent* have been critically acclaimed. So too has the video work of Marlon Riggs and Isaac Julien.[21]

Recognizing the diversity of black gay experience, many black gay critics have sought to read these works in ways that resist homogenizing the lives of black gay men. As Hemphill says in his introduction to *Brother to Brother,* "[i]t would be impossible to say there is one type of black gay male for all seasons. We haven't yet, nor do we need to, become clones."[22] Unfortunately, the dominant culture continues to essentialize black and gay experiences and to ignore almost entirely the lives of those who are both black and gay. As Corbin notes, "the one voice who [has] been our sole, black, openly gay author for four decades [is] James Baldwin."[23]

Another factor contributing to the invisibility of black gay and bisexual authors and books has been the proliferation of chain bookstores, which, with their cheaper prices, greater number of titles, better advertising, and often more convenient locations, squeeze independent bookstores with more diverse selections out of business. Although some of the large chains now include a "Gay Studies" section, a walk through these stores reveals that their selections are often quite minimal and generic, and any publicity they give to gay and bisexual texts tends to highlight only works by a handful of white gay authors.

MAKING THE INVISIBLE VISIBLE IN E. LYNN HARRIS'S INVISIBLE LIFE

With so many factors inhibiting the production of black gay and bisexual literature, the overwhelming success of E. Lynn Harris's novels is surprising.[24] Harris self-published his first novel, *Invisible Life,* in 1991, perhaps for many of the reasons previously discussed. When *Invisible Life* did unexpectedly well (it quickly sold its allotted 10,000 copies), it was reissued by Anchor Books along with Harris's next novel, *Just As I Am,* in 1994. *Invisible Life* centers on the experiences of its narrator, Raymond Tyler, Jr., a southern, Christian, well-educated, middle-class black man who is coming to terms with his bisexual identity. The novel traces the course of his love life, from relationships with Sela and Kelvin at a southern college in Alabama, to subsequent relationships with Quinn and Nicole while a successful attorney in New York City.

Raymond's first relationship with a man occurs early in the novel. While both are in college, his friend Kelvin comes on to him, explaining to Raymond that he is bisexual. After their first sexual experience, Raymond feels a sense of Christian guilt but does not give in to it: "During the altar call I was tempted to throw myself on the altar to repent for Friday night, but I resisted" (24). He and Kelvin begin a secret affair while Raymond continues dating his girlfriend, Sela, who knows nothing of his bisexual behavior. Raymond has intense feelings for both, but finds himself less emotionally intimate with Kelvin: "I thought of the countless times I had told Sela I loved her and really meant it, but I couldn't understand why it was impossible to tell Kelvin just once. Was it possible to be in love with two people at the same time?" (34). Yet, unlike sex with Kelvin, sex with Sela does not entirely satisfy his desires: "Our lovemaking was frequent and passionate, and when I experienced difficulties getting in the mood, I would conjure up thoughts of my lovemaking sessions with Kelvin. It wasn't hurting anyone and Sela seemed satisfied" (30). Raymond's difficulties with Sela seem to stem in part from the lack of sexual intimacy and honesty between them: "I assumed she was satisfied. I sometimes wondered if it wasn't an act. I mean, I had always heard all this stuff about women faking orgasms. At least with Kelvin and me the proof was there" (30). As Raymond has more sexual experiences with men, he increasingly questions his sexual desire not only for Sela, but for any woman:

> I tried to determine the difference between making love with a
> woman and with a man. While I enjoyed this night of passion
> with Sela, I wondered if I had been too methodical in my love-
> making or if I had allowed myself to just let go as I had done so
> many times before with male partners. Was making love to a
> woman now work instead of enjoyment for me? (110)

Raymond continues to search for a sexual identity that is congruent
with his sexual desires when he moves to New York City and encounters his first openly gay black man. He strikes up a friendship with
Kyle, who becomes his "mentor in terms of teaching [him] about the
gay world" (48). Raymond is quick to note the regional differences in
how sexuality is perceived, realizing that New York offers him greater
sexual freedoms than his previous life in Alabama. He observes that
"[d]own South, Kyle would definitely have been labeled a sissy. I told
him on countless occasions that I would have gone in the opposite
direction had I met him in high school or college" (49). New York's
less restrictive atmosphere allows Raymond not only to pursue relationships with men more freely, but also to reconsider his sense of
sexual identity: "I had new friends, a new apartment and a new attitude about life. My life was totally different from the one I had lived
down South. I no longer considered myself straight . . . but was I
completely gay?" (36). At this point, Raymond can begin to imagine
himself with a gay identity, but is still unwilling to entirely sever ties
to heterosexuality.

Although he becomes good friends with Kyle, Raymond remains
closeted. He does not date openly gay men but pursues sexual relationships with other black men who are heterosexually involved. For
example, he begins an affair with Quinn, who is married and the father
of two children. Soon enough, however, Raymond also finds himself
attracted to a Christian black woman named Nicole, and so once again
becomes involved simultaneously with a man and a woman. Quinn
and Raymond share a deep emotional and sexual intimacy, which is
completely invisible to Nicole, as it had been to Sela before. Part of
this intimacy stems from its secrecy, which both Quinn and Raymond
acknowledge: "We talked about how even the smartest of women
couldn't detect undercover gay guys. We also discussed how white

businesspeople never picked up on it either" (132). This secrecy also gives Raymond a sense of power: "It made me realize that in situations like this, men always had the upper hand. They knew about the women in their mates' lives, but the women didn't know about the men in their mates' lives, at least not everything. I knew more about Quinn than his wife did" (179).

But, as Raymond's emotional relationship with Nicole deepens, he becomes less certain about same-sex relationships: "I overheard Nicole tell a friend that since Curtis had become saved, he had given up the homosexual lifestyle. For the first time since my conversion, I wondered if I could change my sexual orientation or at least redirect it. Could you give up the lifestyle and the life? With Nicole, I began to dream old dreams" (175). The language Raymond uses here indicates the discomfort he feels about his bisexual behavior, as well as his difficulty in seeing homosexuality as an acceptable sexual identity. For if, as Raymond wants to believe, homosexuality is merely "a lifestyle," a phrase that resonates with a kind of Christian homophobia, then it is simply a behavior that can be changed or given up.

As much as Raymond tries to convince himself that he loves Nicole and can change, he continues to have more sexually satisfying relationships with men. Eventually, though, Raymond does break off his relationship with Quinn because he is frustrated by Quinn's commitment to his marriage and feels guilty over his own lack of commitment to Nicole. Quinn perceptively responds: "Your desire for me and other men isn't going away because you think you're in love with some woman. I know because I live that lie every day. With the exception of the Saturdays I'm with you" (218). Another reason Raymond ends his relationship with Quinn is because he feels threatened by Quinn's bisexual identity. Uncomfortable with his attraction to men and unwilling to accept his bisexuality, Raymond wants to maintain "that lie" to himself.

And yet, as long as Raymond stays in New York, he continues to encounter bisexual black men who are attracted to him and who remind him of his own conflicted feelings. One of these encounters is with a handsome black football star, Basil Henderson, who is thoughtless, selfish, and homophobic. In his come-on to Raymond at a bar,

Basil reveals both his double life and his ignorance and prejudice regarding black male homosexuality:

> "I *deal* sometimes, but I consider myself straight."
> "Good for you. Then I don't think we have anything else to talk about. . . . So do you consider yourself bisexual?" . . .
> "No, not really."
> "Gay?"
> "Fuck no."
> "Then what did you want to talk with me about?"
> "Well, I like the way you look. I mean, you don't look gay."
> (165-66)

Basil mirrors Raymond's own ambivalence; he dismisses gay and bisexual identities yet desires sexual encounters incongruent with a heterosexual identity. Perhaps because he sees himself in Basil, Raymond rejects his offer.

During this "heterosexual" period of his life, Raymond becomes reacquainted with his first male lover, Kelvin, who is now engaged to Candance, Nicole's best friend. Kelvin tries to persuade Raymond that it would be advantageous for them both to marry and renew their sexual relationship: "I love Candance and I think I can make her happy. Maybe you should consider marrying Nicole and then we could be together forever. . . . I know quite a few guys who are married and still deal with males, but it's usually someone their wife is close to also" (190). Although Raymond rejects Kelvin's offer as well, their sexual history catches up with them when Candance is hospitalized with AIDS-related pneumonia. Candance seems ignorant of Kelvin's bisexual history, even as they get married in the hospital the day before she dies. Nicole, however, recognizes Kelvin's bisexuality, and, because of her violent condemnation of Kelvin's secret behavior and his own feelings of guilt, Raymond discloses his own bisexuality to her. Devastated, she immediately breaks up with him, leading Raymond to contemplate how furtive sexual encounters between men can have dangerous effects on female lovers:

> I was overcome with a tremendous amount of guilt regarding Candance's death. I was part of a secret society that was endan-

gering black women like Candance to protect our secret desires. Would this have happened if society had allowed Kelvin and I to live a life free from ridicule? Was it our fault for hiding behind these women to protect our futures and reputations? What responsibility did these women take? Would they have made the same choices in men had they known everything? With the large number of black bisexual men running the streets, how many lives like Candance's would be snuffed out? (253-54)

Raymond demonstrates here how homophobia within many middle-class black communities contributes to both the sexual secrecy of bisexual black men and the sexual blindness of heterosexual black women. But his argument fails to recognize that IV drug use is often a more significant factor in the spread of HIV among black populations, and the image of a "large number of black bisexual men running the streets," preying on innocent black women and threatening them with AIDS, comes close to reinvoking racist and sexist stereotypes of black male sexuality.

Once Raymond comes out to Nicole, he soon also decides to reveal his sexual feelings for men to his parents. In his conversation with his father, he describes these feelings as his "gayness." His father not only is concerned with how race may complicate Raymond's sexual identity, but wonders too if the city has somehow perverted his son: "You never showed any signs of this when you were a little boy. What about all the girls that called you and what about Sela? Was it New York that changed you? Isn't it tough enough being a black man?" (246). They both feel the threat posed by AIDS, symbolized by Candance's death, and this motivates Raymond's father to accept him, since, as his father says, "I don't want to lose my son to some disease" (247).

Following Candance's death and the end of his relationship with Nicole, Raymond leaves New York, seeking emotional refuge from his problematic love life by returning to Alabama to stay with his parents. Although his parents claim to accept his sexuality, Raymond himself continues to be troubled by it: "I don't know if I thought being back in Alabama would cure my gayness. The opportunities didn't exist as they did in New York" (261). Raymond still perceives his desire for men as simply a problem of sexual behavior–a bad habit that he cannot indulge as easily in Alabama–and decides to try to rid himself of it entirely by committing himself to aiding the larger black community:

> I felt a great deal of responsibility to be a strong role model for my little brother and other young black men. I had to stop beating myself up about my sexual longings. At a time when black men were being maligned, I would concentrate on things that were honorable about me and the qualities that could be an asset to the black community. I felt strongly that I could be of service without people coming into my bedroom. (261-62)

Raymond feels that his "sexual longings" are neither "honorable" nor "an asset" to the black community. The sexual self-hatred expressed in this passage serves as an implicit indictment of members of the black community who are unwilling to accept gay and bisexual black men. In the end, Raymond vows celibacy, hoping to control his desires for men through suppression and by concentrating on the asexual aspects of his identity.

Ultimately, Harris seems to reject bisexuality as an acceptable option for Raymond. Indeed, by the end of the novel, *Invisible Life* seems to act as a criticism of black male bisexuals. Not only is Raymond a fairly unsympathetic character, but the other behaviorally bisexual characters are even less admirable. Kelvin may have killed Candance by infecting her with HIV; Basil is a married homophobe who considers himself straight yet occasionally "deals in trade"; and Quinn, like Basil, lives a life of secret sexual duplicity. Although the novel does not portray a black man who is comfortable with a bisexual identity, it does represent an openly gay black man, Kyle, and, while Raymond has not fully accepted a gay sexual identity by the end of *Invisible Life,* he does seem to be moving away from both heterosexual and bisexual identities. In fact, in Harris's sequel, *Just As I Am,* Raymond acknowledges that he is a gay black man.[25]

As with *Invisible Life,* Harris's later novels, *Just As I Am* (1994) and *And This Too Shall Pass* (1996), use the character of Basil Henderson to portray bisexual black men as duplicitous and possibly dangerous. Indeed, Basil functions as the stereotype of the predatory, married, closeted, bisexual black man. His sexuality seems to symbolize for

Harris the hazardous excessiveness and voracious promiscuity of male bisexuality which threatens to seduce and corrupt monogamous heterosexual relationships.

Surprisingly, in his review of *Just As I Am,* black gay novelist Canaan Parker praises the work for its portrayal of male bisexuality: "The subject of bisexuality gives *Just As I Am* some needed weight–it is a relatively unexplored issue in contemporary gay fiction–and presumably works as well to broaden the cross-over market potential of the novel. . . ."[26] Although Parker finds *Just As I Am* to be "a very commercial novel, both in style and content," he doesn't acknowledge how this commercialism is related to its reiteration of both gay and straight stereotypes of male bisexuality. Additionally, Parker ignores the racial and religious aspects of the novel, which might help explain why he fails to recognize how it vilifies black male bisexuality.[27]

If *Invisible Life* is the story of Raymond's struggle to reject his sexual desires and behavior, *Just As I Am* is the story of Raymond's coming to terms with himself and accepting a gay identity. In his third novel, *And This Too Shall Pass,* Harris continues to portray gay and straight characters who are comfortable with their sexual identities and to villainize the arch-bisexual, Basil Henderson.[28] Unlike Harris's first novel, these works affirm gay and heterosexual identities from the outset and imply that loving relationships can only result from monogamy. Perhaps it is no surprise then that Harris's later novels have been more popular than *Invisible Life*.[29] The only people dismissed and made invisible yet again are those very men whom *Invisible Life* had begun to make visible.

CONCLUSION

The relationship between sexual behavior and sexual identity can be an especially complex one for many black men in the United States, because straight, bisexual, and gay sexual identity categories do not necessarily describe their sexual experiences. Race, class, culture, region, and religion are just a few of the many factors that influence how sexual behavior and identity are linked. With respect to literature, only within the last decade has the literary marketplace become more receptive to the work of black gay men. And only in the last five years, with the publication of E. Lynn Harris's *Invisible Life,* has black male bisexuality become the central theme of an American novel. *Invisible Life* examines the issue of black male bisexual behavior within the context of one man's sexual exploration and development, but it represents this bisexuality as transitional, merely an intermediary step in his psychological growth toward sexual self-identification as a gay black man. Harris's tremendously popular subsequent novels celebrate monogamous relationships but reduce black male bisexuality to a single character who is associated with secrecy and lies.[30]

NOTES

1. E. Lynn Harris, *Invisible Life* (1991; New York: Doubleday, 1994), 206. All further references to the novel will be indicated by parenthesis in the text.

2. Although not the main theme, black male bisexuality had previously been represented in a number of novels by black authors, including Wallace Thurman's *Infants of the Spring,* James Baldwin's *Another Country,* and more subtly, Claude McKay's *Home to Harlem.*

3. Martin F. Manalansan IV, "Double Minorities: Latino, Black, and Asian Men Who Have Sex With Men," *The Lives of Lesbians, Gays and Bisexuals,* eds. Ritch C. Savin-Williams and Kenneth Cohen (Orlando, FL: Harcourt, Brace and Co., 1996), 393. I have found this anthology to be both useful and thorough in its attention to the multiple, connected forces that contribute to the development of human sexualities.

4. The American Psychiatric Association in 1973 and the American Psychological Association in 1975 declassified homosexuality as a medical illness.

5. Theorists from such diverse camps as Kobena Mercer in race theory, Trin T. Min-ha in postcolonialist theory, and Linda Singer in feminist theory have discussed how sexual identity is linked to cultural context. For examples of their work, see Mercer's "Fear of a Black Penis," *Artforum International* 32, no. 8 (April 1994): 74; Min-ha's *Native Woman Other* (Bloomington: Indiana University Press, 1989); and Singer's *Erotic Welfare: Sexual Theory and Politics in the Age of Epidemic* (New York: Routledge, 1993).

6. Benjamin B. Bowser, "Black Men and AIDS: Prevention and Black Sexuality," *The American Black Male: His Present Status and His Future,* eds. Richard G. Majors and Jacob U. Gordon (Chicago: Nelson-Hall, 1994), 121-22.

7. Phillip B. Harper, "Eloquence and Epitaph: Black Nationalism and the Homophobic Impulse in Responses to the Death of Max Robinson," *Writing AIDS: Gay Literature, Language and Analysis,* eds. Timothy F. Murphy and Suzanne Poirier (New York: Columbia University Press, 1993), 124. For more on homophobia and acceptance in black communities, see, for example, bell hooks, "Homophobia in Black Communities," *Talking Back: Thinking Feminist, Thinking Black* (Boston:

South End Press, 1989), 120-26; Jewelle L. Gomez and Barbara Smith, "Taking the Home Out of Homophobia: Black Lesbian Health," *The Black Women's Health Book: Speaking for Ourselves,* ed. Evelyn C. White (Seattle: Seal Press, 1990), 198-213; and Amy Gluckman and Betsy Reed, "Where Has Gay Liberation Gone? An Interview with Barbara Smith," *Homo Economics: Capitalism, Community, and Lesbian and Gay Life,* eds. Gluckman and Reed (New York: Routledge, 1997), 195-207.

8. Laura B. Randolph, "The Hidden Fear: Black Women, Bisexuals and the AIDS Risk," *Ebony,* January 1998: 123.

9. Lynda S. Doll et al., "Male Bisexuality and AIDS in the United States," *Bisexuality and HIV/AIDS: A Global Perspective,* eds. Rob Tielman, Manuel Carballo, and Aart Hendricks (Buffalo, NY: Prometheus Books, 1991), 33.

10. Joseph Beam's *In the Life: A Black Gay Anthology* (Boston: Alyson, 1986) and Essex Hemphill's *Brother to Brother: New Writings by Black Gay Men* (Boston: Alyson, 1991) provide eloquent descriptions by black gay men of the splits they have experienced between their racial and sexual lives.

11. Doll et al., "Male Bisexuality and AIDS in the United States," 34.

12. Charles Stewart, "Double Jeopardy: Black, Gay (and Invisible)," *New Republic,* December 2, 1991: 15.

13. Victoria Brownworth, "Black Out," *The Advocate,* August 13, 1992: 80.

14. Ibid., 80.

15. Ibid., 80.

16. Steven Corbin, "The Dearth of African-American Gay Fiction," *The Advocate,* February 12, 1991: 39.

17. Steven Corbin, "White Men on White Men: The Politics of Publishing and Exclusion," *Lambda Book Report* 3, no. 7 (1992): 4. Corbin's criticism of the racist assumptions about black literature reflect his personal experience and frustrations as a black gay novelist trying to find places willing to publish his work. Although I think he has an important point about the hurdles to publishing black gay novels, I disagree with his easy totalizing of these difficulties to include all black literature. Novels by and about black women have continued to find mass appeal among both black and white audiences, including Terry McMillan's smash hits *Waiting to Exhale* and *How Stella Got Her Groove Back,* both of which were turned into popular Hollywood films. Novels by and about black men, whether gay, straight, or bisexual, have not fared as successfully.

18. Brownworth, "Black Out," 82.

19. Corbin rightly criticizes several leading anthologies of gay fiction edited by white men, including the early volumes of the *Men on Men* series, for their failure to include any work by contemporary black gay men, besides the canonized and deceased token, James Baldwin ("White Men on White Men," 14).

20. Brownworth, "Black Out," 82.

21. Other Countries, *Other Countries: Black Gay Voices; A First Volume* (New York: Other Countries, 1988); B. Michael Hunter, ed., *Sojourner: Black Gay Voices in the Age of AIDS; Other Countries, Volume II* (New York: Other Countries, 1993); Assoto Saint, ed., *The Road Before Us: 100 Gay Black Poets* (New York: Galiens Press, 1991); and Bruce Morrow and Charles H. Rowell, eds., *Shade: An Anthology*

of Fiction by Gay Men of African Descent (New York: Avon Books, 1996). Marlon Riggs's videography includes *Ethnic Notions* (1986), *Tongues Untied* (1991), *Color Adjustment* (1992), and *Black Is, Black Ain't* (1994). Isaac Julien's work includes *Looking for Langston* (1988) and *Young Soul Rebels* (1991).

22. Hemphill, "Introduction," *Brother to Brother,* xxx.

23. Corbin, "White Men on White Men," 14. Ironically, by labeling Baldwin gay, Corbin ignores the fact that Baldwin was behaviorally bisexual.

24. Recently, though, James Earl Hardy's *B-Boy Blues* (Boston: Alyson, 1994) and *2nd Time Around* (Los Angeles: Alyson, 1996) have been positioned in a similar way to Harris's work.

25. E. Lynn Harris, *Just As I Am* (New York: Doubleday, 1994).

26. Canaan Parker, "Review of *Just As I Am,*" *Lambda Book Report* 4, no. 3 (1994): 20.

27. Ibid., 20.

28. E. Lynn Harris, *And This Too Shall Pass* (New York: Doubleday, 1996).

29. When it made its debut, *And This Too Shall Pass* was on *The New York Times Book Review*'s bestseller list for several weeks.

30. U.S. popular culture appears unready for frank depictions of bisexuality of any sort, let alone positive portrayals of bisexuals. The popularity of the movie *Basic Instinct* seems to underscore both the fascination and repulsion that "mainstream" Americans have for even the most normalized and eroticized bisexuality, that of white, wealthy, healthy, young, good-looking women.

How many people can I love at one time?

A lot!

© 2002 by The Haworth Press, Inc. All rights reserved.

[Haworth co-indexing entry note]: "'How Many People Can I Love at One Time? A Lot!" Clurman, Dan. Co-published simultaneously in *Journal of Bisexuality* (Harrington Park Press, an imprint of The Haworth Press, Inc.) Vol. 2, No. 1, 2002, p. 91; and: *Bisexual Men in Culture and Society* (ed: Brett Beemyn and Erich Steinman) Harrington Park Press, an imprint of The Haworth Press, Inc., 2002, p. 91. Single or multiple copies of this article are available for a fee from The Haworth Document Delivery Service [1-800-342-9678, 9:00 a.m. - 5:00 p.m. (EST). E-mail address: getinfo@haworthpressinc.com].

"Ethically Questionable?"

Popular Media Reports on Bisexual Men and AIDS

Marshall Miller

© 2002 by The Haworth Press, Inc. All rights reserved.

[Haworth co-indexing entry note]: "'Ethically Questionable?': Popular Media Reports on Bisexual Men and AIDS." Miller, Marshall. Co-published simultaneously in *Journal of Bisexuality* (Harrington Park Press, an imprint of The Haworth Press, Inc.) Vol. 2, No. 1, 2002, pp. 93-112; and: *Bisexual Men in Culture and Society* (ed: Brett Beemyn and Erich Steinman) Harrington Park Press, an imprint of The Haworth Press, Inc., 2002, pp. 93-112. Single or multiple copies of this article are available for a fee from The Haworth Document Delivery Service [1-800-342-9678, 9:00 a.m. - 5:00 p.m. (EST). E-mail address: getinfo@haworthpressinc.com].

SUMMARY. This article offers an analysis of popular media reports about bisexual men and HIV from some of the first stories about AIDS in the mid-1980s to the present. By not acknowledging the differences between sexual identity and behavior, these reports have stigmatized bisexual men while ignoring the need for safer-sex practices by everyone, regardless of sexual orientation. In addition to this critique, the author suggests alternative strategies for HIV-prevention education. *[Article copies available for a fee from The Haworth Document Delivery Service: 1-800-342-9678. E-mail address: <getinfo@haworthpressinc.com> Website: <http://www.HaworthPress.com> © 2002 by The Haworth Press, Inc. All rights reserved.]*

KEYWORDS. AIDS, biphobia, bisexual men, bisexuality, HIV prevention, media

Even to blasé sophisticates, bisexuality is becoming ethically questionable.

–Martha Smilgis, *Time*[1]

Since I am pretty sure I do not sleep with bisexual men or IV drug users, my main personal concern about AIDS is that men can get the virus from women and subsequently pass it on to other women.

–Meghan Daum, *The New York Times Magazine*[2]

Writing in *The New York Times Magazine* in 1996, Meghan Daum, a 26-year-old, self-identified heterosexual woman, admitted that she regularly had unsafe sex. The above quote illustrates the logic that informs Daum's risk analysis. Consider, for example, the phrase "pretty sure." Could it mean that Daum does not discuss sexual orientation with her partners and that she simply assumes all of them are heterosexual? Or does Daum think she can usually identify and avoid bisexual men? One can only imagine what Daum would do if one of her partners came out to her as bisexual. Would she insist on a condom? Kick him out of bed? Have unsafe sex anyway? Most readers of *The New York Times Magazine* would probably think she was foolish if she had unsafe sex, but if she kicked him out of bed, Daum would be giving in to the sex-phobic, AIDS-paranoid culture she criticizes throughout the article. That leaves the obvious choice of using a condom. But Daum confesses that she fails to practice safer sex in relationships "after the fourth or fifth encounter," feeling that she is not at risk for HIV because of whom she supposedly does and does not have sex with.[3]

Daum's article is just one example of the ways in which bisexual men and HIV prevention are framed in popular culture.[4] My essay examines the mainstream media's treatment of bisexual men within the context of HIV, focusing on how bisexual men are seen as posing a risk to their female partners. I have yet to hear or read about gay men worrying that relationships with bisexual men will place them at a greater risk for HIV than their gay male partners. As I will explain, the reason for these different perceptions is related to the ways in which the spread of HIV has been understood.

My analysis is premised on the understanding that using a condom or dental dam for sex is a very effective method of HIV-risk reduction. Also important to this discussion is recognizing the difference between bisexual identity and behavior–between people who self-identify as bisexual and men who have sex with men and women (MSMW), or women who have sex with women and men (WSWM). A person can identify as heterosexual and have sex with partners of the same gender or identify as gay or lesbian and have sex with partners of another gender. Likewise, a person can self-identify as bisexual and be in a long-term monogamous relationship with one partner.

The distinction between bisexual behavior and identity has critical implications for analyzing HIV risk. Obviously, it is behavior that can place someone at risk for HIV, yet it is identity that is frequently discussed and harshly criticized in the media. The irony here is that a strong sense of identity is often a factor supporting safer-sex behavior. As Peter Chvany states in his study, "Bisexuality and HIV," a "positive self-image is correlated with lower rates of risky behavior."[5] So returning to Daum's hypothetical bisexual partner, should he come out to her as bisexual (and chance being rejected), he may represent a lower risk than someone who insists he is heterosexual, but who in fact has sex with other men. A willingness to disclose sexual orientation may also lead to an increased willingness to disclose HIV status, further empowering women like Daum to protect themselves from HIV.

The popular media reports I will cite illustrate how the cultural narratives of male bisexuality follow the minoritizing/universalizing model that Eve Kosofsky Sedgwick outlines in *Epistemology of the Closet*. Sedgwick writes:

> [there is a] contradiction between seeing homo/heterosexual definition on the one hand as an issue of active importance primarily for a small, distinct, relatively fixed homosexual minority (what I refer to as a minoritizing view), and seeing it on the other hand as an issue of continuing, determinative importance in the lives of people across the spectrum of sexualities (what I refer to as a universalizing view).[6]

Approaches to bisexuality serve as a good example of the tension between universalizing and minoritizing views of identity. Under a universalizing model, the culture imagines that everyone is bisexual, or at least has the potential to be. Thus the extent to which bisexuality is acted upon is a personal decision that all people make. In contrast, a minoritizing model sees a bisexual as a distinct type of person, one who can be located and, if necessary, avoided. Although cultural narratives about identity do not fall entirely on either side of the universalizing/minoritizing split, the contradiction and tension between the extremes, according to Sedgwick, serve as a source of insight and interplay.

THE MAINSTREAM MEDIA "DISCOVERS" BISEXUALITY

After largely ignoring bisexuality in the late 1970s and early 1980s, the mainstream media began to show a greater interest in the topic, culminating in a 1995 *Newsweek* cover story by John Leland entitled "Bisexuality: Not Gay. Not Straight. A New Sexual Identity Emerges."[7] Despite the confusing title (what was "new" about bisexuality?), the article was generally positive; it quoted many self-identified bisexuals, profiled a diverse group of bisexual men and women, and avoided the stereotypical association of bisexuality with AIDS. In particular, the story did not treat bisexual men as a dangerous AIDS threat to heterosexual women, as had earlier magazine articles on bisexuality.[8]

But even when the media is not directly linking bisexuality with AIDS, two prevalent stereotypes of bisexuals affect the public's understanding of HIV transmission. The first is the close association between bisexuality and promiscuity. A common assumption is that bisexuals necessarily have more than one partner, preferably at least one man and one woman. Since monogamy is often considered a primary AIDS prevention strategy, bisexuality seems incompatible with reducing HIV risk. The second stereotype is the media's tendency to reduce bisexuality to a cultural trend. As suggested by Martha Smilgis's reference to "blasé sophisticates" in the quote that opened this essay, the "popularity" of bisexuality is frequently seen as dependent on the amount of cultural support given to it, especially the extent of positive or negative media attention. Therefore, people who insist on identifying as bisexual in the face of the AIDS epidemic and the reports of bisexuals spreading HIV are subject to blame for not "changing their ways" in order to protect themselves and their partners.

The increased hostility toward bisexuality that resulted from AIDS-phobia came during a critical shift in HIV-prevention messages. When AIDS was first identified in the U.S. in the early 1980s, it was considered to be solely a gay men's disease and was called Gay-Related Immune Deficiency (GRID) or the "gay cancer."[9] Because of homophobia and other factors, AIDS was generally ignored at first by the U.S. media and government.[10] But in the mid-1980s, as AIDS was increasingly diagnosed among non-gay population groups, the mainstream media began to take notice, fearing that large numbers of white heterosexuals were at risk. The popular view of AIDS changed from a minoritizing approach to a universalizing one. Sedgwick explains: "AIDS discourse [shifted] with startling rapidity from its previous exclusive and complacent (minoritizing) focus on dangers to distinct 'risk groups' to a much broader, less confident (universalizing) focus on dangers to 'the general public.' . . ."[11]

During this time, the mainstream media also turned its attention to women, who were portrayed as the "innocent victims" of AIDS and warned of the danger posed by bisexual men. The intended female audience for these articles was perhaps best described by a 1995 article in *McCall's*: "Women who never thought they were at risk–people who drive minivans and sing in church choirs–now find themselves taking AZT and tracking T cells."[12] What could be more wholesome and innocent than a minivan and church choir? Inevitably, such reports scrambled for an explanation for how AIDS could travel from gay men and injection drug users to people not in so-called "high-risk groups." Bisexual men were seen as the logical link and became an easy target for blame.

One way in which this blame model worked was to focus on the story of a white, heterosexual woman who learned that she was HIV positive by surprise. Using a minoritizing model of bisexuality, the media reported on how the woman then went searching for answers and discovered the secret bisexual life of her male partner. Examples of this trend abound. In a report on long-term AIDS survivors in *Parade Magazine,* the author, Bernard Gavzer, told the story of Niro Asistent, a Bridgehampton, New York, woman living with AIDS.[13] Gavzer described how Asistent became ill in 1985 and was diagnosed with AIDS-related complex, or ARC (a diagnosis that is no longer used). "I couldn't figure out how it happened to me," Asistent said. Gavzer cleared up the mystery for the curious reader: "When her lover fell ill, she got the answer: He was bisexual. He soon died of AIDS."[14] In Gavzer's narrative, the bisexual is used to explain the intrusion of AIDS into the "safe" space of Asistent's white (the magazine includes a photo of her), straight life. Because the story was about long-term survivors, perhaps Gavzer saw it as only appropriate that, at the time of publication, Asistent was still living, but the bisexual man, who was not named, had already died.

An article in the *Los Angeles Times* with the headline "Hidden Dangers" told a similar story: "When Doug DeFord died of AIDS in 1990, Marie DeFord was mystified. Doug was a married man, and he wasn't an IV drug user. But when DeFord emptied her husband's wallet soon after his death, she found two membership cards to gay bathhouses in a nearby city. Suddenly it all made sense." DeFord herself added, "I had no idea my husband was bisexual–none. . . . He played Russian roulette with my life and lost."[15] While we can assume that Doug DeFord had sex with other men, there is no evidence that he ever identified as bisexual. Admittedly, such a distinction probably does not matter to Marie DeFord. But imagine another man, who is questioning whether he should come out to his wife as bisexual. One of the reasons why people do not identify as bisexual is because of biphobia–the fear and hatred of bisexuals. This article is not going to make men who have sex with men think, "I'm bisexual too. I should come out to my wife." When bisexuals are represented as dangerous, dishonest people to be avoided at all costs, there is much less incentive for men who have sex with both men and women to identify as bisexual.

While the point of Marie DeFord's story is that there could be a Doug DeFord equivalent in every marital bedroom, the point of the story of Alison Gertz, another woman infected by a man who had sex with other men, is much more complex. Unlike DeFord, Gertz became a media icon, one of the public faces of HIV, along with Rock Hudson, Magic Johnson, and Ryan White. Gertz's tale has been told many times, from the cover of *People* to *Oprah* to *The New York Times* to a made-for-TV movie. As a result, there are many versions of her story, with varying degrees of accuracy. But because it is a moral fable, the lesson is considered more important than the details of the plot.

One version of Gertz's story, an article by *The New York Times* reporter Gina Kolata entitled "Teenagers + AIDS," appeared in 1990 in *Seventeen,* a popular magazine marketed to young women. Most of the first paragraph of the story was enlarged to fill the page, heightening the impact of the opening words: "For Alison Gertz, the shock and surprise that she had AIDS came when she was twenty-three, seven years after she had sexual intercourse, just once, on a romantic, moonlit night, with a man infected with the AIDS virus. The man, she learned, has since died of the disease."[16] The reader is not told anything more about the man; even his name, Cort Brown, was apparently considered of little importance.

Other media reports were somewhat more descriptive; they characterized Brown as bisexual, including another article written by Kolata, this time for *Ladies' Home Journal,* which appeared several months prior to the *Seventeen* story. Entitled "Women and AIDS: What You Must Know Now," the article began with a photo of Gertz along with the caption: "Alison Gertz, a twenty-three-year-old New York illustrator who is bright and successful, contracted AIDS, she believes, from having sex just once with a bisexual man."[17] The addition of the word "bisexual" here completely changes the moral of Gertz's story. For the *Seventeen* audience, the message is "sex can kill you." However, for the "ladies" of *Ladies' Home Journal,* it is "bisexual men can kill you, even if you sleep with them just once."

Besides Brown's alleged bisexuality, the version aimed at younger women also did not mention that Brown wooed her with gifts of champagne and roses.[18] Perhaps this suggestion of underage drinking was seen as tarnishing the young, "innocent victim" image that *Seventeen* sought to present. Certainly, this would have been the case had either article disclosed that Gertz met him in Studio 54, where he worked as a bartender, and that drug use preceded their sexual encounter. According to Katie Roiphe, in her book *Last Night in Paradise: Sex and Morals at the Century's End,* "Later Alison would amend her account of the 'romantic' night: 'He was so coked out, he just couldn't have an orgasm. . . . The sex was terrible.'"[19]

In her articles, Kolata reveals little about Gertz's life, beyond the fact that she "grew up in a wealthy Park Avenue family" and "never suspect[ed] that AIDS was something that could happen to someone like her."[20] Indeed, there is no reason why she should have known. She and Cort Brown spent their one night together in 1982, when HIV was little understood and hardly covered in the mainstream press and long before the media shifted its focus from AIDS as the gay cancer to AIDS as a potential risk to everyone.[21]

In HIV researchers' eyes, Gertz's experience is an anomaly. She was infected during her only sexual encounter with Brown, at a time when the vast majority of infections occurred among men who had sex with men and injection drug users. So why then did Kolata write two stories about her and turn this isolated case into every woman's potential threat from HIV? And why did Gertz become a symbol of AIDS for both *Seventeen* and *Ladies' Home Journal*? For Kolata and the magazines' editors, Gertz probably represents whom they think of as their typical reader. She is white, comes from a wealthy family, and had sex because the conditions seemed right–it was a romantic, moonlit night. Despite the subsequent revelations of drinking and drug use, Gertz also seemingly represents an "innocent victim" because she likely had sex before knowing about AIDS. She did not grow up inundated with AIDS information, as did many of the women reading about her experience seven years later. Gertz's story serves as a metaphor, a media fable about what supposedly happens to women who have sex when they are 16 years old (for *Seventeen* readers) or who have sex with bisexual men (for *Ladies' Home Journal* readers). Kolata emphasizes this last point by concluding:

> [A woman] can reduce her chances [of becoming infected with HIV] to one in five *billion* if her partner is at lowest risk–meaning he uses a condom, is not bisexual, promiscuous or an intravenous drug-user, did not receive a blood transfusion between 1978 and 1985–*and* if he is tested and found free of the AIDS virus.[22]

This quote sums up the stereotypical message imparted to *Ladies' Home Journal* readers about how to reduce their risk. Using a condom is simple, straightforward, logical advice. But instead of empowering women to insist that all of their male partners use condoms, the decision is portrayed as the man's choice. It is as if a woman is expected to bring a man home, see if he puts on a condom, and then decide if he is a high or low risk based on his actions. As for the final item on the list, a person who is not infected with HIV is obviously not going to transmit HIV. However, given the window period between infection and a positive test result, condom use remains the best HIV-risk reduction advice.

Of course, ensuring that someone remains uninfected through sexual contact requires a commitment to either safer sex or monogamy, neither of which Kolata seems to think bisexual men are capable of. She is not alone in this belief, for the mainstream media typically represents bisexuality as if nonmonogamy were endemic to its nature. For example, in his *Newsweek* cover story on bisexuality, John Leland wrote: "In a culture organized, however precariously, around monogamy, bisexuality lurks as a rupture in the social structure, conjuring fears of promiscuity, secret lives, and instability." To emphasize this point, a summation of the quote appears in large print at the top of the page: "To a social order based on monogamy, bisexuality looms as a potent threat."[23]

Although Leland accurately recognizes that "failed monogamy is already a principal source of pain in this country," he is more critical of bisexuality for "suggest[ing] that nonmonogamy, or 'polyamory,' is an accepted part of life."[24] Polyamory, though, is a satisfying way of life not just for a number of bisexuals, but for people of all sexual orientations, who make an open, honest, mutual choice to have a nonmonogamous relationship. Yet, because of their association with nonmonogamy, only bisexuals have become scapegoats for unsuccessful monogamous relationships among heterosexuals.

Of course, nonmonogamy is not a necessary aspect of bisexuality. As Paula Rust states in the *Newsweek* article: "Imagine concluding that a person who finds both blue and brown eyes attractive would require two lovers, one with each eye color, instead of concluding that this person would be happy with *either* a blue-eyed or a brown-eyed lover." Even Leland himself begrudgingly admits that "[i]n practice[,] promiscuity is not an article of faith for all bisexuals; it's an option. Many bis are monogamous for all or parts of their lives."[25] Still, by using the word "promiscuity" here instead of "nonmonogamy," Leland continues to emphasize that bisexuals who have sex with more than one partner, especially partners of more than one gender, have indiscriminant sexual relations. But a person can be nonmonogamous and still be selective when choosing partners–because someone does not categorically limit their involvement to one partner does not mean they have sex with "anything that moves." Consider, for example, the difference between serial monogamy and long-term polyamory. In the first situation, a person could be monogamous, but have three partners over the course of three years. In the latter situation, a person could be nonmonogamous and also have three partners in three years. Same number of partners, same time period, yet only the polyamorous person would likely be considered promiscuous by Leland and many other mainstream media journalists.[26]

But the *Newsweek* article does differ from many other media reports in that it extensively quotes self-identified bisexuals, not just the "experts" who have studied them or non-bisexuals who have had a negative experience with someone bisexual. An example of this latter case is Jon Nordheimer's front-page story, "AIDS Specter for Women: The Bisexual Man," in *The New York Times* on April 3, 1987. The article begins in typical bisexual male AIDS-scare fashion, using the experiences of one heterosexual woman to serve as a warning to all women: "Seven years ago a Miami office worker had an affair with a bisexual man. She recalls that his confusion about sexual orientation was one of the things that made her feel tender toward him. Now she wonders if she should get a blood test for the AIDS virus."[27] In just three sentences, Nordheimer manages to invoke many of the prevalent myths about male bisexuality: bisexual men are confused about their sexuality, engage in unprotected sex with many partners, and likely spread AIDS. Never mind that this woman's relationship was in 1980, before AIDS was identified in the U.S., or that she was probably more at risk from unprotected sex with her presumably heterosexual male partners since then. Nordheimer is only concerned about the supposed threat that bisexual men pose to heterosexual women.

The article does explain that, statistically, more women have been infected by intravenous drug users than by bisexual men.[28] But injection drug users are seemingly of little interest to the largely white middle- and upper-class women who read *The New York Times,* because of false assumptions about the race and social class of drug users. Instead, the reader is told:

> [for] a middle-class woman who thinks the chance of contact with a drug addict using contaminated needles is remote[,] . . . the figure of the male bisexual, cloaked in myth and his own secretiveness, has become the bogyman of the late 1980's, casting a chill on past sexual encounters and prospective ones.
>
> She might also be distressed to learn that bisexuals are often secretive and complex men who, experts say, probably would not acknowledge homosexual activity even if questioned about it. Indeed, some cannot even admit such behavior to themselves.[29]

This quote sets the tone for the article and demonstrates how Nordheimer demonizes bisexual men in order to be able to blame someone for heterosexual women having to worry about HIV and the sexual history of their partners. As Sedgwick notes:

> This male-authored article mobilizes and ferments the anxiety and uncertainty, as it appropriates the actual voices, of women who supposedly *have to know* all the secrets of men's sexuality–so that, apparently, they can avoid having any sex with bisexual men and have unprotected sex with certifiably heterosexual men. This *having to know* is artificially constructed in the article, which is carefully framed to omit the obvious, epistemologically relaxing option that these women might choose to use care and condoms in all their sexual contacts at this point.[30]

As part of this process of "having to know," Nordheimer groups bisexual men into different categories: (1) married men leading "clandestine homosexual lives"; (2) men who are "promiscuous only in their homosexual orientation" but "interact with women in a sporadic, serial manner"; (3) men "unsettled by identity confusion" who jump back and forth between men and women; and (4) "young men who experiment with homosexuality in college or some other environment where it is tolerated or easy to hide."[31]

Nordheimer also describes a fifth category of bisexual men, but gives them a different name: "'ambisexuals,' a small but 'dangerous' group of men who have very frequent sexual contact with both men and women."[32] Here is the classic stereotype of bisexuals as having sex with "anything that moves," a position espoused in the article by Laud Humphreys, a Los Angeles psychotherapist known for his controversial studies of men who have sex with other men in public restrooms. According to Humphreys, ambisexuals "don't care if a partner is a man or a woman as long as that person is good-looking and sexually active," and because they are supposedly unable to control themselves, he sees these bisexuals as representing the greatest HIV risk. "I consider this group the most dangerous in the cross-infection of AIDS because these men are likely to be drug-abusers as well, overlapping their high-risk behavior."[33] Note the language of contagion with the words "cross-infection" and "overlapping." The phrase "most dangerous," of course, refers not to the risk these men face themselves if they have unprotected sex, but the seeming threat they pose to their partners. Like gay men, bisexual men are often seen as expendable in the AIDS epidemic. It does not matter if they die, as long as they do not infect their female partners or, more accurately, as long as they do not have female partners.

The fear of so-called ambisexuals could also result from anxiety over the universalizing model of bisexuality–that if most people are potentially bisexual and willing to have sex with both women and men, this could be a leading cause of HIV transmission. Such anxiety is readily apparent in Martha Smilgis's 1987 article, "The Big Chill: Fear of AIDS," in *Time* magazine. Throughout the story, Smilgis paints a grim portrait of sex, particularly bisexuality, which she sees as a dangerous practice that AIDS is causing to go out of style. She quotes Monica Feinberg, "a heterosexual Yale graduate," who "maintains that bisexual dating, which was not only accepted but chic among some students at certain Ivy League colleges, is no longer exciting and fun." Because "[i]t was mostly experimentation . . . [t]he students do not consider themselves bisexual . . . They felt that sleeping around was no longer a novelty." Smilgis suggests that "the problem of bisexuality is especially poignant in the world of arts and entertainment, where sexual exoticism in general is more tolerated than in society as a whole." While she warns of the dangers of AIDS, seemingly hoping for a world in which bisexuality is not "tolerated" and no longer a "problem," Smilgis provides no scientific evidence that bisexual men are a major conduit of HIV infection to heterosexual women. Bisexuality, rather than unsafe sexual practices, becomes "ethically questionable."[34]

REPRESENTATIONS OF BISEXUAL MEN AND AIDS TODAY

I began this essay with a 1996 quote from Meghan Daum, which I refer to again to demonstrate that such biphobic rhetoric continues today. It is not a coincidence that some of the most vehement biphobia arose at the same time that the mainstream media was cautioning heterosexual America about the dangers posed by HIV. While there is no question that these warnings should have been made, the problem lies with how they were made. Bisexual men–and to a lesser extent, injection drug users–were scapegoated and blamed for the transmission of HIV to heterosexual women. The popular press sought to portray women as the victims of irresponsible, deceitful bisexual men who had too much sex with too many people. But as sex-positive members of the gay community have shown, AIDS does not mean that people need to stop having sex with gay and bisexual men, enjoy it less, or have an irrational fear of it. It does mean, however, that people need to practice safer sex.

In recent years, the media's biphobia about HIV and AIDS is often less blatant, but even more commonplace. In particular, warnings about the dangers of bisexual men have become part of the fabric of HIV-prevention messages for heterosexual women. For example, in the 1995 *McCall's* article about women and AIDS, a section entitled "Lowering Your Odds" offered as its first suggestion: "Avoid high-risk sexual partners. As well as people diagnosed with HIV or AIDS, these include bisexual men and IV-drug users."[35] Yet again, bisexuality equals HIV.

These messages shape the attitudes of health care providers and AIDS service agency personnel, people who are in a position to know better. Consider, for example, the experiences of women who admit to having bisexual partners when being tested for HIV. In a pre-test counseling session, one woman was urged by the tester to end her relationship with the man immediately. In another, a tester told a woman that she was at high risk for HIV because bisexual men could not be trusted.[36] Neither counselor was concerned about the man's HIV status or the couple's safer-sex practices. As I have demonstrated throughout this essay, bisexual men are often considered to be a distinct category of people whose behavior is more dangerous and deceitful than heterosexual men. But since when have straight men been entirely trustworthy?

The dominant society has long conflated same-sex desire with illness, so that for many people, AIDS has merely reaffirmed what they believed all along. Anal sex is especially seen as "unnatural, offensive, and illness-linked," which, as Eric Rofes notes, has a number of important ramifications.[37] First, this view reaffirms that those who engage in acts of homosexual sodomy (a phrase often used, even by the Supreme Court, to describe male-male sex[38]) will be punished by becoming sick. Second, it leads to the expectation that, because anal sex is considered unnatural and outside the norm, it can be easily replaced with other activities in the face of HIV. Third, in a homophobic society, people who have no concern for gay men who transmit HIV to other gay men suddenly become infuriated at the thought of bisexual men passing HIV along to their female partners.

Bisexual men, along with other men, should use condoms. Unfortunately, it is the need for condom use by non-bisexual men, particularly heterosexual men, that is forgotten in the rush to condemn bisexual men for their relationships with heterosexual women. In the mainstream media, only bisexual men are untrustworthy; either they choose to be bisexual because it is trendy, or they hide their identities and spread HIV because they are unwilling to warn their partners of their promiscuous ways.

Because there have been and will continue to be instances where women are infected with HIV by men who have sex with both men and women, how can the media play a positive role in prevention and education? As a first step, news stories should distinguish between identity and behavior, such as by recognizing the fact that many self-identified lesbians and gay men have had sex with someone of a different gender in the recent past.[39] Given that sexual experience cannot be assumed to match identity, the articles should address the need for people of all genders and sexual orientations to practice safer sex, instead of stigmatizing specific identities. Moreover, they should acknowledge the existence of both self-identified bisexuals and people who have sex with women and men. Currently, the media conflates these two groups and fails to recognize that each has its own unique prevention and education needs.

Stories should also include interviews with and quotes from bisexual men, not just the wives and lovers of dead ones. These men could discuss their experiences of coming to terms with their bisexuality and of coming out to their partners. Some would be HIV positive, others

HIV negative. Some would be monogamous, others would be in honest, open relationships in which safer sex was practiced outside the primary relationship(s). These articles would recognize the value of portraying stigmatized identities in a positive light, particularly since HIV-risk behavior is often related to self-esteem. They would list local bisexual resources, such as support groups, Web sites, and social events.

These media reports would provide risk-reduction information for bisexual men and their partners and offer models that encourage people to practice safer sex, regardless of the gender or sexual orientation of their partners, such as by presenting effective strategies for negotiating condom use. Readers would also learn about the experiences of heterosexual women who are in satisfying relationships with bisexual men and hear the voices of bisexual women, who are currently ignored in media reports on bisexuality and HIV.

Finally, these media reports would give people of all sexual orientations tips and tools for discussing sexuality with their partners, from sexual orientation to sexual experience to safer sex. They would spark bedroom and dining room conversations about sex and risk and how to make the difficult decisions. The media would be part of the process of empowering people to protect themselves from HIV, instead of promoting biphobia.

NOTES

1. Martha Smilgis, "The Big Chill: Fear of AIDS," *Time*, February 16, 1987: 53.

2. Meghan Daum, "Safe-Sex Lies," *The New York Times Magazine*, January 21, 1996: 33.

3. Ibid., 32.

4. Many of the articles discussed in this essay were found using Lexis-Nexis, a comprehensive, computer-based legal and news database. Lexis-Nexis enables a wide range of newspapers and magazines to be searched through the use of keywords. Given the strength of this method, I believe that the articles cited are representative of popular media reports on bisexual men and AIDS during this time.

5. Peter Chvany, "Bisexuality and HIV: An Overview," slide presentation at "Playing Safe with Both Teams: Bisexuality and HIV Prevention" Conference, June 21, 1999, Boston.

6. Eve Kosofsky Sedgwick, *Epistemology of the Closet* (Berkeley: University of California Press, 1990), 1.

7. John Leland, "Bisexuality: Not Gay. Not Straight. A New Sexual Identity Emerges," *Newsweek,* July 17, 1995: 47. Ironically, *Newsweek* had proclaimed the emergence of bisexuality more than two decades earlier; "Bisexual Chic: Anyone Goes," *Newsweek,* May 27, 1974: 90.

8. In addition to the articles discussed in this essay, magazine stories that portray bisexual men as a major AIDS threat to heterosexual women include Anne Conover Heller, "Is There a Man in Your Man's Life?: What Every Girl Should Know about the Bisexual Guy," *Mademoiselle,* July 1987: 134-35, 153-54; Susan Gerrard and James Halpin, "The Risky Business of Bisexual Love," *Cosmopolitan,* October 1989: 202-05; Esther Davidowitz, "The Secret Life of Bisexual Husbands," *Redbook,* September 1993: 114-17, 135.

9. The *Impact of Homophobia and Other Social Biases on AIDS: A Special Report by Public Media Center* (San Francisco: Public Media Center, 1995).

10. The Public Media Center report makes an excellent comparison between AIDS and Legionnaire's Disease in terms of the amount of media and government attention given to both in the early days of each epidemic. According to the report, "[b]y the end of 1982, two years into the epidemic, and with 634 cases of the fatal illness reported–most of them in the city of New York–*The New York Times* had printed a total of only six articles on the epidemic, none of them on the front page. This is in contracts to the 33 articles–11 of them on the front page–that *The New York Times* had printed during the first 30 days of the Legionnaire's Disease outbreak, when the illness's death toll had reached 24" (Ibid., 8).

11. Sedgwick, *Epistemology of the Closet,* 249.

12. Debra Kent, "Could the Woman Next Door Have AIDS?," *McCall's,* February 1995: 63.

13. Bernard Gavzer, "Love Has Helped Keep Me Alive," *Parade Magazine,* April 16, 1995: 4.

14. Ibid., 6.

15. Ann Japenga, "Hidden Dangers: Worried by AIDS Threat, Experts Focus on Bisexual Men Who Put Themselves, Families at Risk," *Los Angeles Times,* May 21, 1992: E1.

16. Gina Kolata, "Teenagers + AIDS," *Seventeen,* May 1990: 148.

17. Gina Kolata, "Women and AIDS: What You Must Know Now," *Ladies' Home Journal,* November 1989: 98.

18. Ibid., 100.

19. Katie Roiphe, *Last Night in Paradise: Sex and Morals at the Century's End* (New York: Random House, 1997), 47.

20. Kolata, "Women and AIDS," 100, and "Teenagers + AIDS," 149.

21. Still, what Gertz apparently found attractive about Brown was a sense of risk. "There was a nebulousness surrounding his life, unlike the boys she went to school with who complained about their English teachers, went with their families to the same sort of summer places, and drove the same sort of cars," writes Roiphe. "What was stirring was the unknown." Roiphe attributes the unknown and nebulous aspects of Cort Brown to the class differences between them. "For the young Alison Gertz, part of the bartender's thrill was that he *was* a bartender. He lived somewhere outside

the large, airy, highly upholstered Park and Fifth Avenue apartments of her friends." Roiphe, *Last Night in Paradise,* 47-48.

22. Kolata, "Women and AIDS," 102. Kolata is citing an analysis by Norman Hearst and Stephen B. Hulley, both epidemiologists at the University of California, San Francisco.

23. Leland, "Bisexuality," 47.

24. Ibid., 47.

25. Ibid., 47.

26. The perceived linkage between bisexuality and promiscuity has also served as a main point of attack against bisexuals by right-wing fundamentalists. For example, in arguing against the Employment Non-Discrimination Act, Robert Knight claimed that "ENDA is bad legislation because it . . . [p]uts the federal government officially in support of promiscuity since bisexuals by definition have sex with more than one person." Robert Knight, "Prelude to Sexual Legal Anarchy?," *The Washington Times,* August 22, 1996: A15.

27. Jon Nordheimer, "AIDS Specter for Women: The Bisexual Man," *The New York Times,* April 3, 1987: A1.

28. For more information on bisexual men and HIV infection, see Joseph P. Stokes, Kittiwut Taywaditep, Peter Vanable, and David J. McKirnan, "Bisexual Men, Sexual Behavior, and HIV/AIDS," *Bisexuality: The Psychology and Politics of an Invisible Minority,* ed. Beth A. Firestein (Thousand Oaks, CA: Sage Publications, 1996), 149. I do not mention this fact in order to shift the blame to injection drug users, but rather as a way of acknowledging how this issue works in a cultural economy where most of the anxiety about bisexual men arises from the fact that they could be anywhere, hiding without track marks on their arms–a visual marker that the dominant society believes can be used to single out and isolate injection drug users.

29. Nordheimer, "AIDS Specter for Women," A1, D18.

30. Sedgwick, *Epistemology of the Closet,* 249-50.

31. Nordheimer, "AIDS Specter for Women," D18.

32. Ibid., D18.

33. Ibid., D18.

34. Smilgis, "The Big Chill," 52.

35. Kent, "Could the Woman Next Door Have AIDS?," 68.

36. These incidents took place in Rhode Island in the mid-1990s.

37. Eric Rofes, *Reviving the Tribe: Regenerating Gay Men's Sexuality and Culture in the Ongoing Epidemic* (Binghamton, NY: Harrington Park Press, 1996), 103, 144.

38. See the 1986 Supreme Court decision in *Bowers v. Hardwick.* This case is analyzed in great detail in William B. Rubenstein, ed., *Lesbians, Gay Men, and the Law* (New York: The New Press, 1993).

39. Recent studies have found that 81% of self-identified lesbians and bisexual women have had sex with a man in the last three years, and two-thirds of young gay men have had sex with a woman–21% in the previous three months. Among the lesbians and bisexual women who had sex with men, 39% had unprotected vaginal sex and 11% had unprotected anal sex. The Lesbian AIDS Project of Massachusetts, *Lesbians and HIV* (Boston); Lynda Richardson, "Study Finds HIV Infection Is High for

Young Gay Men," *The New York Times,* February 16, 1999: B4; Beryl Koblin, Lucia Torian et al., "High HIV-1 Seroprevalence Among Young Men Who Have Sex with Men (MSM) in New York City," presentation at the 6th Conference on Retroviruses and Opportunities Infections, February 2, 1999, Chicago; personal communication with Lucia Torian and Beryl Koblin.

Index

© 2001 by The Haworth Press, Inc. All rights reserved.